tulip doctrines

Five Sermons by C. H. Spurgeon

TABLE OF CONTENTS

T – Total Depravity

U – Unconditional Election

L – Limited (Or Particular) Atonement

I – Irresistible Grace

P – Perseverance of the Saints

Praise for *tulip doctrines*

"Spurgeon once remarked that Calvinism is just a nickname for Christianity. And from his pulpit, here are five sermons from the Prince of Preachers on Christianity. The late great theologian Dr. John H. Gerstner often referred to TULIP as 'the loveliest flower in all of God's garden.' Here is that lovely flower gloriously arrayed by one of its most able defenders."

Dr. Don Kistler
Founder, Soli Deo Gloria and
The Northampton Press

T

Total

Depravity

THE CARNAL MIND ENMITY AGAINST GOD

A SERMON DELIVERED ON LORD'S DAY
MORNING,
APRIL 22, 1855,
BY C. H. SPURGEON,

AT EXETER HALL STRAND

"The carnal mind is enmity against God."
Romans 8:7.

This is a very solemn indictment which the
Apostle Paul here speaks against the carnal
mind. He declares it to be enmity against God.
When we consider what man once was, only
second to the angels, the companion of God,
who walked with Him in the Garden of Eden in
the cool of the day. When we think of him as
being made in the very image of his Creator,
pure, spotless and unblemished, we cannot
but feel bitterly grieved to find such an
accusation as this declared against us as a
race. We may well hang our harps upon the
willows while we listen to the voice of Jehovah,
solemnly speaking to His rebellious creature—
"How are you fallen from Heaven, you son of
the morning!" "You seal up the sum, full of
wisdom and perfect in beauty. You have been
in Eden, the Garden of God. Every precious

stone was your covering—the workmanship of your fleshly tabrets and of your pipes was prepared in you in the day that you were created. You are the anointed cherub that covers and I have set you so—you were upon the holy mountain of God. You have walked up and down in the midst of the stones of fire. You were perfect in your ways from the day that you were created, till iniquity was found in you and you sinned. Therefore I will cast you as profane out of the mountain of God— and will destroy you, O covering cherub, from the midst of the stones of fire."

There is much to sadden us in a view of the ruins of our race. As the Carthaginian who might tread the desolate site of his much-loved city would shed many tears when he saw it laid in heaps by the Romans. Or as the Jew, wandering through the deserted streets of Jerusalem, would lament that the plowshare had marred the beauty and the glory of that city which was the joy of the whole earth. So ought we to mourn for ourselves and our race when we behold the ruins of that goodly structure which God has made—that creature, matchless in symmetry, second only to angelic intellect, that mighty being, man—when we behold how he is "fallen, fallen, fallen, from his high estate" and lies in a mass of destruction.

A few years ago a star was seen blazing out with considerable brilliance but soon disappeared. It has since been affirmed that it was a world on fire, thousands of millions of miles from us and yet the rays of the conflagration reached us. The noiseless messenger of light gave to the distant dwellers on this globe the alarm of, "A world on fire!" But what is the conflagration of a distant planet, what is the destruction of the mere material of the most ponderous orb compared with this fall of humanity, this wreck of all that is holy and sacred in ourselves? To us, indeed, the things are scarcely comparable, since we are deeply interested in one, though not in the other. The Fall of Adam was OUR fall. We fell in and with him. We were equal sufferers. It is the ruin of our own house that we lament. It is the destruction of our own city that we bemoan when we stand and see written in lines too plain for us to mistake their meaning, "The carnal mind"—that very same mind which was once holiness and has now become carnal—"is enmity against God." May God help me this morning to solemnly speak this indictment against you all! Oh, that the Holy Spirit may so convince us of sin that we may unanimously plead "guilty" before God!

There is no difficulty in understanding my text—it needs scarcely any explanation. We all know that the word "carnal" here signifies "fleshly." The old translators rendered the passage thus—"The mind of the flesh is enmity against God." That is to say, the natural mind—that soul which we inherit from our fathers—that which was born within us when our bodies were fashioned by God. The fleshly mind, the lusts, the passions of the soul, it is this which has gone astray from God and become enmity against Him!

But before we enter upon a discussion of the Doctrine of the text, observe how strongly the Apostle expresses it. "The carnal mind," he says, "it is ENMITY against God." He uses a noun and not an adjective. He does not say it is merely opposed to God, but it is positive enmity! It is not black, but blackness. It is not *at* enmity, but *enmity* itself. It is not corrupt, but corruption. It is not rebellious, it is rebellion—it is not wicked, it is wickedness itself. The heart, though it is deceitful, is positively deceit. It is evil in the concrete, sin in the essence. It is the distillation, the quintessence of all things that are vile. It is not envious against God, it is *envy*. It is not *at* enmity, it is *actual enmity*.

Nor need we say a word to explain that it is "enmity *against* God." It does not charge manhood with an aversion merely to the dominion, Laws, or Doctrines of Jehovah. It strikes a deeper and surer blow. It does not strike man upon the head but it penetrates into his heart. It lays the axe at the root of the tree and pronounces man, "enmity *against* God." Against the Person of the Godhead, against the Deity, against the mighty Maker of this World—not at enmity against His Bible or against His Gospel—though that is true, but against God Himself; against His Essence, His Existence and His Person! Let us, then, weigh the words of the text, for they are solemn words. They are well put together by that master of eloquence, Paul. They were, moreover, dictated by the Holy Spirit, who tells man how to speak aright. May He help us to expound, as He has already given us the passage to explain.

We shall be called upon to notice this morning, first, *the truthfulness of this assertion.* Secondly, *the universality of the evil here complained of.* Thirdly, we will still further enter into the depths of the subject and press it to your hearts, by showing *the enormity of the evil.* And after that, should we have time, we will deduce one or two Doctrines from the general fact.

I. First, we are called upon to speak of *the truthfulness of this great statement,* "the carnal mind is enmity against God." It needs no proof, for since it is written in God's Word, we, as Christian men and women, are bound to bow before it. The words of the Scriptures are words of infinite wisdom and if reason cannot see the ground of a statement of Revelation, it is bound, most reverently, to believe it, since we are well-assured, even should it be above our reason, that it cannot be contrary to it! Here I find it written in the Scriptures, "the carnal mind is enmity against God." And that, of itself, is enough for me. But did I need witnesses, I would conjure up the nations of antiquity. I would unroll the volume of ancient history, I would tell you of the awful deeds of mankind. It may be I might move your souls to detestation if I spoke of the cruelty of this race to itself, if I showed you how it made the world an Aceldama by its wars and deluged it with blood by its fights and murders! If I should recite the black list of vices in which whole nations have indulged or even bring before you the characters of some of the most eminent philosophers, I would blush to speak of them and you would refuse to hear. Yes, it would be impossible for you, as refined inhabitants of a civilized country, to endure the mention of the crimes that were committed by those very men who nowadays are held up as being paragons of perfection! I fear if all the truth were written, we should rise up from reading the lives of earth's mighty heroes and proudest sages and would say at once of all of them, "They are clean gone mad! They are altogether become unprofitable. There is none that does good. No, not one!"

And did not that suffice, I would point you to the delusions of the heathen. I would tell you of their priestcraft by which their souls have been enthralled in superstition. I would drag their gods before you. I would let you witness the horrid obscenities, the diabolical rites which are to these besotted men most sacred things! Then, after you had heard what the natural *religion* of man is, I would ask what must his *irreligion* be? If this is his devotion, what must be his impiety? If this is his ardent love of the Godhead, what must his hatred thereof be? You would, I am sure, at once confess, did you know what the race is, that the indictment is proven and that the world must unreservedly and truthfully exclaim, "guilty."

A further argument I might find in the fact that the best of men have been always the most ready to confess their depravity. The holiest men, the most free from impurity, have always felt it most. He whose garments are the whitest will best perceive the spots upon them. He whose crown shines the brightest will know when he has lost a jewel. He who gives the most light to the world will always be able to discover his own darkness. The angels of Heaven veil their faces. And the angels of God on earth, His chosen people, must always veil their faces with humility when they think of what they were! Hear David—he was none of those who boast of a holy nature and a pure disposition. He says, "Behold, I was shapen in iniquity; and in sin did my mother conceive me." Hear all those holy men who have written in the Inspired Volume and you shall find them all confessing that they were not clean, no, not one. Yes, one of them even exclaimed, "O wretched man that I am! who shall deliver me from the body of this death?"

And more—I will summon one other witness to the truthfulness of this act who shall decide the question. It shall be your conscience. Conscience, I will put you in the witness box and cross-examine you this morning! Conscience, answer truly! Be not drugged with the opium of self-security! Speak the truth! Did you ever hear the heart say, "I wish there were no God?" Have not all men, at times, wished that our religion were not true? Though they could not entirely rid their souls of the idea of the Godhead, did they not wish that there might not be God? Have they not had the desire that it might turn out that all these Divine realities were a delusion, a farce? "Yes," says every man, "that has crossed my mind sometimes. I have wished I might indulge in folly. I have wished there were no laws to restrain me. I have wished, as the fool, that there were no God." That passage in the Psalms, "The fool has said in his heart, there is no God," is wrongly translated. It should be, "The fool has said in his heart, *no God*." The fool does not say in his heart *there is* no God, for he knows there is a God. Rather he says, "No God—I don't want any, I wish there were none." And who among us has not been so foolish as to desire that there were no God? Now, Conscience, answer another question! You have confessed that you have at times wished there were no God. Now, suppose a man wished another dead, would not that show that he hated him? Yes, it would. And so, my Friends, the wish that there were no God proves that we dislike God! When I wish such a man dead and rotting in his grave, when I desire that he were *non est*, I must hate that man—otherwise I would not wish him to be extinct. So that wish—and I do not think there has been a man in this world who has not had it—proves that "the carnal mind is enmity against God."

But, Conscience, I have another question. Has not your heart ever desired, since there *is* a God, that He were a little less holy, a little less pure—so that those things which are now great crimes might be regarded as venial offenses, as peccadilloes? Has your heart ever said, "Would to God these sins were not forbidden. Would that He would be merciful and pass them by without an atonement! Would that He were not so severe, so rigorously just, so sternly strict to His integrity." Have you never said that, my Heart? Conscience must reply, "you have." Well, that wish to *change* God proves that you are not in love with the God that now is—the God of Heaven and earth! And though you may talk of natural religion and boast that you do reverence to the God of the green fields, the grassy meads, the swelling flood, the rolling thunder, the azure sky, the starry night and the great universe—though you love the poetic ideal of Deity, it is not the God of Scripture— for you have wished to change His nature and in that you have proved that you are at enmity with Him! So where do we go from here? You can bear faithful witness if you would speak the truth that each person here has so transgressed against God, so continually broken His Laws, violated His Sabbath, trampled on His statutes, despised His Gospel, that it is true, yes, most true, that "the carnal mind is enmity against God."

II. Now, secondly, we are called upon to notice the *universality of this evil.* What a broad assertion it is! It is not a single carnal mind, or a certain class of characters, but "*the* carnal mind." It is an unqualified statement including every individual. Whatever mind may properly be called carnal, not having been spiritualized by the power of God's Holy Spirit, is "enmity against God."

Observe then, first of all, the universality of this as to *all persons.* Every carnal mind in the world is at enmity against God! This does not exclude even infants at the mother's breast. We call them innocent and so they are of actual transgression, but as the poet says, "Within the youngest breast there lies a stone." There is in the carnal mind of an infant enmity against God. It is not developed, but it lies there. Some say that children learn sin by imitation. But no—take a child away, place it under the most pious influences, let the very air it breathes be purified by piety—let it constantly drink in draughts of holiness. Let it hear nothing but the voice of prayer and praise. Let its ears be always kept in tune by notes of sacred song—and that child, notwithstanding, may still become one of the grossest of transgressors! And though placed apparently on the very road to Heaven, it shall, if not directed by Divine Grace, march downwards to the pit of Hell! Oh, how true it is that some who have had the best of parents have been the worst of children—that many who have been trained up under the most holy auspices, in the midst of most favorable scenes of piety—have, nevertheless, become loose and wanton! So it is not by imitation but it is by *nature* that the child is evil! Grant me that the child is carnal and my text says, "The carnal mind is enmity against God." The young crocodile, I have heard, when broken from the shell, will in a moment begin to put itself in a posture of attack, opening its mouth as if it had been taught and trained. We know that young lions, when tamed and domesticated, will still have the wild nature of their fellows of the forest and were liberty given them, would prey as fiercely as others. So with the child. You may bind him with the green withes of education, you may do what you will with him—but you cannot change his heart! That carnal mind shall still be at enmity against God. And notwithstanding intellect, talent and all you may give to boot, it shall be of the same sinful complexion as every other child, if not as apparently evil, for "the carnal mind is enmity against God."

And if this applies to children, equally does it include every class of men. There are some men who are born into this world master spirits. They walk about it as giants, wrapped in mantles of light and glory. I refer to the poets—men who stand aloft like Colossi—mightier than we, seeming to be descended from celestial spheres. There are others of acute intellect, who, searching into mysteries of science, discover things that have been hidden from the creation of the world! Men of keen research and mighty erudition—and yet of each of these—poet, philosopher, metaphysician and great discoverer—it can be said, "The carnal mind is enmity against God." You may train him up, you may make his intellect almost angelic, you may strengthen his soul until he shall take what are riddles to us and unravel them with his fingers in a moment. You may make him so mighty that he can grasp the iron secrets of the eternal hills and grind them to atoms in his fist. You may give him an eye so keen that he can penetrate the deep secrets of rocks and mountains. You may add a soul so potent that he may slay the giant Sphinx that had, for ages, troubled the mightiest men of learning. Yet when you have done all this, his mind shall be a depraved one and his carnal heart shall still be in opposition to God. Yes, more, you may bring him to the

House of Prayer. You may make him sit constantly under the clearest preaching of the Word of God where he shall hear the Doctrines of Grace in all their purity, attended by a holy unction. But if that holy unction does not *rest upon him*, all shall be vain—he shall attend most regularly, but like the pious door of the Chapel that turns in and out, he shall still be the same—having an outside superficial religion and his carnal mind shall still be at enmity against God. Now, this is not my assertion, it is the declaration of God's Word, and you must leave it if you do not believe it! But quarrel not with me, it is my Master's message and it is true of every one of you— men, women and children and myself, too— that if we have not been regenerated and converted, if we have not experienced a change of heart, our carnal mind is still at enmity against God!

Again, notice the universality of this at *all times*. The carnal mind is at *all times* enmity against God. "Oh," say some, "it may be true that we are at times opposed to God, but surely we are not *always* so." "There are moments," says one, "when I feel rebellious. At times my passions lead me astray. But surely there are other favorable seasons when I really am friendly to God and offer true devotion. I have (continues the objector) stood upon the mountaintop, until my whole soul has kindled with the scene below and my lips have uttered the song of praise—

"These are Your glorious works, parent of good,
Almighty, Yours this universal frame,
Thus wondrous fair—Yourself how wondrous then!"

Yes, but mark—what is true one day is not false another, "the carnal mind is enmity against God" at all times! The wolf may sleep, but it is still a wolf. The snake with its azure hues may slumber amid the flowers and the child may stroke its slimy back, but it is still a serpent. It does not change its nature, though it is dormant. The sea is the house of storms even when it is glassy as a lake. The thunder is still the mighty rolling thunder when it is so much aloft that we hear it not. And the heart, when we perceive not it's boiling, when it belches not forth its lava and sends not forth the hot stones of its corruption, is still the same dread volcano! At all times, at all hours, at every moment, (I speak this as God speaks it) if you are carnal, you are each one of you enmity against God!

Another thought concerning the universality of this statement: *The whole of the mind* is enmity against God. The text says, "The carnal mind is enmity against God," that is, the entire man, every part of him—every power, every passion. It is a question often asked, "What part of man was injured by the Fall?" Some think that the Fall was only felt by the affections and that the intellect was unimpaired. This they argue from the wisdom of man and the mighty discoveries he has made, such as the law of gravity, the steam engine and the sciences. Now I consider these things as being a very mean display of wisdom, compared with what is to come in the next hundred years—and very small compared with what might have been if man's intellect had continued in its pristine condition. I believe the Fall crushed man entirely! Albeit, when it rolled like an avalanche upon the mighty temple of human nature, some shafts were still left undestroyed and amidst the ruins you find here and there a flute, a pedestal, a cornice, a column not quite broken—yet the entire structure fell and its most glorious relics are fallen ones, leveled in the dust. The whole of man is defaced. Look at *our memory*—is it not true that the memory is fallen? I can recollect evil things far better than those which savor of piety. I hear a ribald song—that same music of Hell shall jar in my ear when gray hairs shall be upon my head! I hear a note of holy praise—alas, it is forgotten! Memory grasps with an iron hand ill things, but the good she holds with feeble fingers. She allows the glorious timbers from the forest of Lebanon to swim down the stream of oblivion, but she stops all the dross that floats from the foul city of Sodom! She will retain evil, she will lose good. Memory is fallen. So are the *affections*. We love everything earthly better than we ought. We soon fix our heart upon a creature but very seldom upon the Creator. And when the heart is given to Jesus it is prone to wander. Look at the *imagination*, too. Oh, how can the imagination revel when the body is in an ill condition! Only give man something that shall well near intoxicate him. Drug him with opium and how his imagination will dance with joy! Like a bird uncaged, how will it mount with more than eagles' wings! He sees things he had not dreamed of even in the shades of night. Why did not his imagination work when his body was in a normal state—when it was healthy? Simply because it is depraved! And until he had entered a foul element—until the body had begun to quiver with a kind of intoxication—the fancy would not hold its carnival. We have some splendid specimens of what men could write when they have been under the accursed influence of ardent spirits. It is because the mind is so depraved that it loves something which puts the body into an abnormal condition. And here we have proof that the imagination, itself, has gone astray. So with the *judgment*—I might prove how ill it decides. So might I accuse the *conscience* and tell you how blind it is and how it winks at the greatest follies. I might review all our powers and write upon the brow of each one, "Traitor against Heaven! Traitor against God!" The whole "carnal mind is enmity against God."

Now, my Hearers, "the Bible, alone, is the religion of Protestants"—but whenever I find a certain book much held in reverence by our Episcopalian brethren, entirely on my side, I always feel the greatest delight in quoting from it. Do you know I am one of the best Churchmen in the world, the very best, if you will judge me by the Articles and the very worst if you measure me in any other way? Measure me by the Articles of the Church of England and I will not stand second to any man under Heaven's blue sky in preaching the Gospel contained in them! For if there is an excellent epitome of the Gospel it is to be found in the Articles of the Church of England. Let me show you that you have not been hearing strange Doctrine. Here is the 9th Article, upon Original or Birth Sin. "Original Sin stands not in the following of Adam (as the Pelagians do vainly talk) but it is the fault and corruption of the nature of *every man* that naturally is engendered of the offspring of

Adam. Whereby man is very far gone from original righteousness, and is of his own nature inclined to evil, so that the flesh lusts always contrary to the spirit. And, therefore, in every person born into this world, it deserves God's wrath and damnation. And this infection of nature does remain, yes, in them that are regenerated, whereby the lust of the flesh, called in the Greek, *phronema sarkos* which some do expound the wisdom, some sensuality, some the affection, some the desire of the flesh, is not subject to the Law of God. And although there is no condemnation for them that believe and are baptized, yet the Apostle does confess that concupiscence and lust has of itself the nature of sin. I need nothing more! Will anyone who believes in the Prayer Book dissent from the Doctrine that "the carnal mind is enmity against God"?

III. I have said that I would endeavor, in the third place, to show the great *enormity of this guilt*. I do fear, my Brothers and Sisters, that very often when we consider our state, we think not so much of the guilt as of the misery. I have sometimes read sermons upon the inclination of the sinner to evil in which it has been very powerfully proven and certainly the pride of human nature has been well humbled and brought low. But one thing always strikes me, if it is left out, as being a very great omission—the Doctrine that man is *guilty* in all these things! If his heart is against God, we ought to tell him it is *his sin.* And if he cannot repent we ought to show him that sin is the sole cause of his disability—that all his alienation from God is sin—that as long as he keeps from God it is sin! I fear many of us here must acknowledge that we do not charge the sin of it to our own consciences. Yes, we say, we have many corruptions. Oh, yes. But we sit down very contented. My Brothers and Sisters, we ought not to do so. Having those corruptions is our crime which should be confessed as an enormous evil. If I, as a minister of the Gospel, do not press home the sin of the thing, I have missed what is the very virus of it. I have left out the very essence if I have not shown that it is a crime. Now, "the carnal mind is enmity against God." What a sin it is! This will appear in two ways. Consider the relation in which we stand to God and then remember what God is. And after I have spoken of these two things, I hope you will see, indeed, that it is a sin to be at enmity with God!

What is God to us? He is the Creator of the heavens and the earth. He bears up the pillars of the universe, His breath perfumes the flowers. His brush paints them. He is the Author of this fair creation. "We are the sheep of His pasture, He has made us and not we ourselves." He stands to us in the relationship of a Maker and Creator—and from that fact He claims to be our King. He is our Legislator, our Law-Maker. And then, to make our crime still worse and worse, He is the Ruler of Providence, for it is He who keeps us daily. He supplies our needs. He keeps the breath within our nostrils. He bids the blood still pursue its course through the veins. He holds us in life and prevents us from death. He stands before us, our Creator, our King, our Sustainer, our Benefactor. And I ask, is it not a sin of enormous magnitude—is it not high treason against the Emperor of Heaven—is it not an awful sin, the depth of which we cannot fathom with the line of all our judgment—that we, His creatures, dependent upon Him, should be at enmity with Him?

But the crime may be seen to be worse when we think of *what God is*. Let me appeal personally to you in an interrogatory style, for this has weight with it. Sinner! Why are you at enmity with God? God is the God of Love. He is kind to His creatures. He regards you with His love of benevolence. This very day His sun has shone upon you. This day you have had food and raiment and you have come up here in health and strength. Do you hate God because He loves you? Is that the reason? Consider how many mercies you have received at His hands all your lives long! You are born with a body not deformed, you have had a tolerable share of health. You have been recovered many times from sickness. When lying at the gates of death, His arm has held back your soul from the last step to destruction. Do you hate God for all this? Do you hate Him because He spared your life by His tender mercy? Behold His goodness that He has spread before you! He might have sent you to Hell, but you are here. Now, do you hate God for sparing you? Oh, why are you at enmity with Him? My fellow creature, do you not know that God sent His Son from His bosom, hung Him on the tree and there allowed Him to die for sinners, the Just for the unjust? And do you hate God for that? Oh, Sinner, is this the cause of your enmity? Are you so estranged that you give enmity for love? And when He surrounds you with favors, girds you with mercies, encircles you with lovingkindness, do you hate Him for this? He might say as Jesus did to the Jews— "For which of these works do you stone Me?" For which of these works do you hate God? If an earthly benefactor fed you, would you hate him? If he clothed you, would you abuse him to his face? If he gave you talents, would you turn those powers against him? Oh, speak! Would you forge the iron and strike the dagger into the heart of your best friend? Do you hate your mother who nursed you on her knee? Do you curse your father who so wisely watched over you? No, you say, we have some little gratitude towards earthly relatives. Where are your hearts, then? Where are your hearts that you can still despise God and be at enmity with Him? Oh, diabolical crime! Oh, Satanic enormity! Oh, iniquity for which words fail in description! To hate the All-Lovely—to despise the essentially Good—to abhor the constantly Merciful—to spurn the Ever-Beneficent—to scorn the King, the Gracious One! Above all, to hate the God who sent His Son to die for man! Ah, in that thought—"the carnal mind is enmity against God"—there is something which may make us shake. For it is a terrible sin to be at enmity with God. I wish I could speak more powerfully, but only my Master can impress upon you the enormous evil of this horrid state of heart!

IV. But there are one or two Doctrines which we will try to deduce from this. Is the carnal mind at "enmity against God?" Then *salvation cannot be by merit*, it must be by Grace. If we are at enmity with God, what merit can we have? How can we deserve anything from the Being we hate? Even if we were pure as Adam, we could not have any merit. For I do not think Adam had any desert before his Creator. When he had kept all his Master's Law, he was but an unprofitable servant. He had done no more than he ought to have done. He had no surplus—no balance. But since we have become enemies, how much less can we hope to be saved by works! Oh, no. The whole Bible tells us, from beginning to end, that salvation is not by the works of the Law but by the deeds of Grace. Martin Luther declared that he constantly preached justification by faith alone, "because," he said, "the people would forget it—so that I was obliged almost to knock my Bible against their heads to send it into their hearts." So it is true we constantly forget that salvation is by Grace alone. We always want to be putting in some little scrap of our own virtue. We want to be *doing* something. I remember a saying of old Matthew Wilkes— "Saved by your works? You might as well try to go to America in a paper boat!" Saved by your works? It is impossible! Oh no! The poor legalist is like a blind horse going round and round the mill, or like the prisoner going up the treadmill and finding himself no higher after all he has done. He has no solid confidence, no firm ground to rest upon. He has not done enough—never enough. Conscience always says, "this is not perfection. It ought to have been better." Salvation for enemies must be by an ambassador—by an Atonement—yes, by Christ.

Another Doctrine we gather from this is *the necessity of an entire change of our nature.* It is true that by birth we are at enmity with God. How necessary, then, it is that our *nature* should be *changed.* There are few people who sincerely believe this. They think that if they cry, "Lord, have mercy upon me," when they lie a-dying, they shall go to Heaven directly. Let me suppose an impossible case for a moment. Let me imagine a man entering Heaven without a change of heart. He comes within the gates. He hears a sonnet. He starts! It is to the praise of his *Enemy.* He sees a Throne and on it sits One who is glorious, but it is his *Enemy.* He walks streets of gold, but those streets belong to his *Enemy.* He sees hosts of angels, but those hosts are the servants of his *Enemy.* He is in his *Enemy's* house, for he is at *enmity* with God! He could not join the song, for he would not know the tune. There he would stand—silent, motionless—till Christ should say, with a voice louder than ten thousand thunders, "What are *you* doing here? Enemies at a marriage banquet? Enemies in the children's house? Enemies in Heaven? Get you gone! Depart, you cursed, into everlasting fire in Hell!" Oh, Sirs, if the unregenerate man could enter Heaven, I mention once more the oft-repeated saying of Whitefield, "he would be so unhappy in Heaven that he would ask God to let him run down into Hell for shelter." There must be a *change* if you consider the future state. For how can enemies of God ever sit down at the banquet of the Lamb?

And to conclude, let me remind you—and it is in the text, after all—that *this change must be worked by a power beyond your own*. An enemy may possibly make himself a friend, but *enmity* cannot. If it is but an adjunct of his nature to be an enemy he may change himself into a friend. But if it is the very *essence* of his existence to be enmity, positive enmity, enmity cannot change itself. No, there must be something done more than we can accomplish. This is just what is forgotten in these days. We must have more preaching of the Holy Spirit if we are to have more conversion work. I tell you, Sirs, if you change yourselves and make yourselves better and better and better, a thousand times, you will never be good enough for Heaven! Till God's Spirit has laid His hand upon you. Till He has renewed your heart—till He has purified your soul, till He has changed your entire spirit and made you a new man— there can be no entering Heaven. How seriously, then, should each stand and think, "Here am I, a creature of a day, a mortal born to die, but yet an immortal! At present I am at enmity with God. What shall I do? Is it not my duty, as well as my happiness, to ask whether there is a way to be reconciled to God?"

Oh, weary slaves of sin, are not your ways the paths of folly? Is it wisdom, O my fellow creatures—is it wisdom to hate your Creator? Is it wisdom to stand in opposition against Him? Is it prudent to despise the riches of His Grace? If it is wisdom, it is Hell's wisdom! If it is wisdom, it is a wisdom which is folly with God! Oh, may God grant that you may turn unto Jesus with full purpose of heart! He is the Ambassador. He it is who can make peace through His blood. And though you came in here an enemy, it is possible you may go out through that door a friend—if you can but look to Jesus Christ, the brazen serpent which was lifted up!

And now, it may be, some of you are convinced of sin by the Holy Spirit. I will now proclaim to you the way of salvation. "As Moses lifted up the serpent in the wilderness, even so must the Son of Man be lifted up—that whoever believes in Him should not perish, but have eternal life." Behold, O trembling penitent, the means of your deliverance! Turn your tearing eyes to yonder Mount of Calvary. I see the Victim of Justice—the Sacrifice of Atonement for your transgression! View the Savior in His agonies, with streams of blood purchasing your soul and with most intense agonies enduring your punishment. He died for *you*, if now you confess your guilt! O come, you condemned one, self-condemned—turn your eyes this way, for one look will save! Sinner, you are bitten. Look! It is nothing but "Look!" It is simply, "Look!" If you can but look to Jesus you are safe! Hear the voice of the Redeemer—"Look unto Me and be you saved." Look! Look! Look! O guilty souls—

> ***"Venture on Him, venture wholly,***
> ***Let no other trust intrude!***
> ***None but Jesus***
> ***Can do helpless sinners good!"***

May my blessed Master help you to come to Him and draw you to His Son, for Jesus' sake. Amen and Amen.

U

Unconditional Election

UNCONDITIONAL ELECTION

A SERMON DELIVERED ON LORD'S DAY MORNING,
SEPTEMBER 2, 1855,
BY C H. SPURGEON,

AT NEW PARK STREET CHAPEL,
SOUTHWARK.

"But we are bound to give thanks alway to God for you,
brethren beloved of the Lord, because God hath
from the beginning chosen you to salvation through sanctification of the Spirit and belief of the truth:
Whereunto he called you by our gospel, to the obtaining
of the glory of our Lord Jesus Christ."
2 Thessalonians 2:13, 14

IF there were no other text in the Sacred Word except this one, I think we would all be bound to receive and acknowledge the truthfulness of the great and glorious Doctrine of God's ancient choice of His family. But there seems to be an inveterate prejudice in the human mind against this Doctrine—and although most other Doctrines will be received by professing Christians, some with caution, others with pleasure—this one seems to be most frequently disregarded and discarded! In many of our pulpits it would be reckoned a high sin and treason to preach a sermon upon *Election* because they could not make it what they call a, "practical" discourse! I believe they have erred from the Truth of God. Whatever God has revealed, He has revealed for a purpose. There is nothing in Scripture which may not, under the influence of God's Spirit, be turned into a practical discourse—"for all Scripture is given by inspiration of God and is profitable" for some purpose of spiritual usefulness. It is true, it may not be turned into a free will discourse—that we know right well—but it *can* be turned into a practical Free *Grace* discourse. And Free Grace practice is the best practice when the true Doctrines of God's Immutable Love are brought to bear upon the hearts of saints and sinners! Now I trust, this morning, some of you who are startled at the very sound of this word will say, "I will give it a fair hearing. I will lay aside my prejudices. I will hear what this man has to say." Do not shut your ears and say at once, "It is high Doctrine." Who has authorized you to call it high or low? Why should you oppose yourself to God's Doctrine? Remember what became of the children who found fault with God's Prophet and exclaimed, "Go up, you bald-head! Go up, you bald-head!" Say nothing against

God's Doctrines, lest haply some evil beast should come out of the forest and devour you also! There are other woes beside the open judgment of Heaven—take heed that these fall not on your head. Lay aside your prejudices—listen calmly, listen dispassionately—hear what Scripture says! And when you receive the Truth, if God should be pleased to reveal and manifest it to your souls, do not be ashamed to confess it! To confess you were wrong yesterday is only to acknowledge that you are a little wiser today. Instead of being a reflection on yourself, it is an honor to your judgment and shows that you are improving in the knowledge of the Truth of God! Do not be ashamed to learn and to cast aside your old doctrines and views, but take up that which you may more plainly see to be in the Word of God. And if you do not see it to be here in the Bible—whatever I may say, or whatever authorities I may plead—I beseech you, as you love your souls, reject it! And if from this pulpit you ever hear things contrary to this Sacred Word, remember that the Bible must be first—and God's minister must lie underneath it!

We must not stand on the Bible to preach—we must preach with the Bible above our heads. After all we have preached, we are well aware that the mountain of Truth is higher than our eyes can discern—clouds and darkness are round about its summit and we cannot discern its topmost pinnacle. Yet we will try to preach it as well as we can. But since we are mortal and liable to err, exercise your judgment—"Try the spirits, whether they are of God"—and if on mature reflection on your bended knees, you are led to disregard Election—a thing which I consider to be utterly impossible—then forsake it! Do not hear it preached, but believe and confess whatever you see to be God's Word. I can say no more than that by way of introduction.

Now, first, I shall speak a little concerning the *truthfulness* of this Doctrine—"God has from the beginning chosen you to salvation." Secondly, I shall try to prove that this Election is *absolute*—"He has from the beginning chosen you to salvation," not for sanctification, but, "*through sanctification* of the Spirit and belief of the truth." Thirdly, this Election is *eternal* because the text says, "God has from *the beginning* chosen you." Fourthly, it is *personal*—"*He* has chosen *you*." Then we will look at the *effects* of the Doctrine—see what it does. And lastly, as God may enable us, we will try and look at its *tendencies* and see whether it is, indeed, a terrible and licentious Doctrine. We will take the flower and, like true bees, see whether there is any honey whatever in it—whether any good can come *of* it—or whether it is an unmixed, undiluted evil.

I. First, I must try and prove that the Doctrine is TRUE. And let me begin with an *argumentum ad hominem*—I will speak to you according to your different positions and stations. There are some of you who belong to the Church of England and I am happy to see so many of you here, though now and then I certainly say some very hard things about Church and State, yet I love the old Church, for she has in her communion many godly ministers and eminent saints. Now I know you are great Believers in what the Articles declare to be sound Doctrine. I will give you a specimen of what they utter concerning Election, so that if you believe them, you cannot avoid receiving Election. I will read a portion of the 17th Article upon Predestination and Election—

"Predestination to life is the everlasting purpose of God, whereby (before the foundations of the world were laid) He has continually decreed by His counsel, secret to us, to deliver from curse and damnation those whom He has chosen in Christ out of mankind and to bring them by Christ to everlasting salvation, as vessels made to honor. Therefore, they which are endued with so excellent a benefit of God, are called according to God's purpose by His Spirit working in due season: they, through Divine Grace, obey the calling: they are justified freely: they are made sons of God by adoption: they are made like the image of His only-begotten Son Jesus Christ: they walk religiously in good works and at length, by God's mercy, they attain to everlasting felicity."

Now, I think any Churchman, if he is a sincere and honest believer in Mother Church, must be a thorough believer in Election. True, if he turns to certain other portions of the Prayer Book, he will find things contrary to the Doctrines of Free Grace and altogether apart from Scriptural teaching. But if he looks at the Articles, he must see that God has chosen His people unto eternal life! I am not so desperately enamored, however, of that book as you may be—and I have only used this Article to show you that if you belong to the Establishment of England, you should at least offer no objection to this Doctrine of Predestination.

Another human authority whereby I would confirm the Doctrine of Election is the old Waldensian Creed. If you read the creed of the old Waldenses—emanating from them in the midst of the burning heat of persecution—you will see that these renowned professors and confessors of the Christian faith did most firmly receive and embrace this Doctrine as being a portion of the Truth of God. I have copied from an old book, one of the Articles of their faith—"That God saves from corruption and damnation those whom He has chosen from the foundations of the world, not for any disposition, faith, or holiness that He before saw in them, but of His mere mercy in Christ Jesus, His Son, passing by all the rest according to the irreprehensible reason of His own free will and justice."

It is no novelty, then, that I am preaching no new Doctrine! I love to proclaim these strong old Doctrines which are called by nickname, Calvinism, but which are surely and verily the revealed Truth of God as it is in Christ Jesus! By this Truth of God, I make a pilgrimage into the past and as I go, I see father after father, confessor after confessor, martyr after martyr standing up to shake hands with me! Were I a Pelagian, or a believer in the Doctrine of free will, I would have to walk for centuries all alone. Here and there a heretic of no very honorable character might rise up and call me Brother. But taking these things to be the standard of my faith, I see the land of the ancients peopled with my Brothers and Sisters—I behold multitudes who confess the same as I do and acknowledge that this is the religion of God's own Church!

I also give you an extract from the old Baptist Confession. We are Baptists in this congregation—the greater part of us at any rate—and we like to see what our own forefathers wrote. Some 200 years ago the Baptists assembled together and published their articles of faith to put an end to certain reports against their orthodoxy which had gone forth to the world. I turn to this old book—which I have just published—Baptist Confession of Faith—and I find the following as the Third Article—"By the decree of God, for the manifestation of His Glory, some men and angels are predestinated, or foreordained, to eternal life through Jesus Christ to the praise of His glorious Grace; others being left to act in their sin to their just condemnation to the praise of His glorious Justice. These angels and men, thus predestinated and foreordained, are particularly and unchangeably designed, and their number so certain and definite that it cannot be either increased or diminished. Those of mankind who are predestinated to life, God, before the foundation of the world was laid, according to His eternal and Immutable purpose and the secret counsel and good pleasure of His will, has chosen in Christ unto everlasting glory out of His mere Free

47

Grace and love, without any other thing in the creature as condition or cause moving Him hereunto."

As for these human authorities, I care not one rush for all three of them! I care not what they say, pro or *con*, as to this Doctrine. I have only used them as a kind of confirmation to *your* faith, to show you that while I may be railed upon as a heretic and as a hyper-Calvinist, after all I am backed up by antiquity! All the past stands by me. I do not care for the present. Give me the past and I will hope for the future. Let the present rise up in my teeth, I will not care, even though a host of the Churches of London may have forsaken the great cardinal Doctrines of God, it matters not. If a handful of us stand alone in an unflinching maintenance of the Sovereignty of our God, if we are beset by enemies, yes, and even by our own Brothers and Sisters who ought to be our friends and helpers, it matters not if we can but count upon the past, the noble army of martyrs, and the glorious host of confessors! They are our friends. They are the witnesses of the Truth of God and they stand by us! With these for us, we will not say that we stand alone, but we may exclaim, "Lo, God has reserved unto Himself seven thousand that have not bowed the knee unto Baal." But the best of all is—*God* is with us!

The great Truth of God is always the Bible and the Bible alone. My Hearers, you do not believe in any other book than the Bible, do you? If I could prove this from all the books in Christendom—if I could fetch back the Alexandrian library and prove it there—you would not believe it any the more! But you surely will believe what is in God's Word!

I have selected a few texts to read to you. I love to give you a whole volley of texts when I am afraid you will distrust a Truth of God so that you may be too astonished to doubt! Just let me run through a catalog of passages where the people of God are called elect. Of course if the people are called *elect*, there must be *Election*. If Jesus Christ and His Apostles were accustomed to call Believers by the title of elect, we must certainly believe that they were so, otherwise the term does not mean anything! Jesus Christ says, "Except that the Lord had shortened those days, no flesh should be saved: but for the *elect's* sake, whom He has chosen, He has shortened the days." "False Christs and false Prophets shall rise, and shall show signs and wonders, to seduce, if it were possible, even the *elect*." "Then shall He send His angels and shall gather together His elect from the four winds, from the uttermost part of the earth to the uttermost part of Heaven."—Mark 13:20, 22,

27. "Shall not God avenge His own *elect* which cry day and night unto Him, though He bear long with them?"—Luke 18:7. Many other passages might be selected wherein the word, "elect," or, "chosen," or, "foreordained," or "appointed," is mentioned, or the phrase, "My sheep," or some similar designation, show that Christ's people are distinguished from the rest of mankind!

But you have concordances and I will not trouble you with texts. Throughout the Epistles the saints are constantly called, "the elect." In Colossians we find Paul saying, "Put on therefore, as the *elect* of God, holy and beloved, bowels of mercies." When he writes to Titus, he calls himself, "Paul, a servant of God and an Apostle of Jesus Christ, according to the faith of God's *elect*." Peter says, "*Elect* according to the foreknowledge of God the Father." Then if you turn to John, you will find he is very fond of the word! He says, "The elder to the *elect* lady." And he speaks of our "*elect* sister." And we know where it is written, "The church that is at Babylon, *elected* together with you." They were not ashamed of the word in *those* days. They were not afraid to talk about it. Nowadays the word has been dressed up with diversities of meaning and persons have mutilated and marred the Doctrine so that they have made it a very Doctrine of devils! I do confess that many who call themselves Believers have gone to rank Antinomianism! But notwithstanding this, why should I be ashamed of it if men wrest it? We love God's Truth on the rack as well as when it is walking upright. If there were a martyr whom we loved before he went on the rack, we would love him still more when he was stretched there! When God's Truth is stretched on the rack, we do not call it a lie! We love not to see it racked, but we love it even when racked because we can discern what its proper proportions ought to have been if it had not been racked and tortured by the cruelty and inventions of men! If you will read many of the Epistles of the ancient fathers, you will find them always writing to the people of God as the "elect." Indeed, the common conversational term used among many of the Churches by the primitive Christians to one another was that of the "elect." They would often use the term to one another, showing that it was generally believed that all God's people were manifestly "elect."

But now for the verses that will positively prove the Doctrine. Open your Bibles and turn to John 15:16, and there you will see that Jesus Christ has chosen His people, for He says, "You have not chosen Me, but I have chosen you, and ordained you, that you should go and bring forth fruit, and that your fruit should remain: that whatsoever you shall ask of the Father in My name, He may give it you." Then in the 19th verse, "If you were of the world, the world would love his own, but because you are not of the world, but I have chosen you out of the world, therefore the world hates you." Then in the 17th Chapter and the 8th and 9th verses, "For I have given unto them the words which You gave Me; and they have received them, and have known surely that I came out from You, and they have believed that You did send Me. I pray for them: I pray not for the world, but for them which You have given Me; for they are Yours." Turn to Acts 13:48—"And when the Gentiles heard this, they were glad, and glorified the Word of the Lord: and as many as were ordained to eternal life believed." They may try to split that passage into hairs if they like—but it says, "ordained to eternal life" in the original as plainly as it possibly can! And we do not care about all the different commentaries thereupon. You scarcely need to be reminded of Romans 8, because I trust you are all well-acquainted with that Chapter and understand it by this time. In the 29th and following verses, it says, "For whom He did foreknow, He also did predestinate to be conformed to the image of His Son, that He might be the firstborn among many Brethren. Moreover whom He did predestinate, them He also called: and whom He called, them He also justified: and whom He justified, them He also glorified. What shall we then say to these things? If God is for us, who can be against us? He that spared not His own Son, but delivered Him up for us all, how shall He not with Him also freely give us all things? Who shall lay anything to the charge of God's elect?" It would also be unnecessary to repeat the whole of the 9th Chapter of Romans. As long as that remains in the Bible, no man shall be able to prove Arminianism! So long as that is written there, not the most violent contortions of the passage will ever be able to exterminate the Doctrine of Election from the Scriptures! Let us read such verses as these— "For the children being not yet born, neither having done any good or evil, that the purpose of God according to Election might stand, not of works, but of Him that calls; it was said unto her, The elder shall serve the younger." Then read the 22nd verse, "What if God, willing to show His wrath, and to make His power known, endured with much longsuffering the vessels of wrath fitted to destruction? And that He might make known the riches of His glory on the vessels of mercy, which He had afore prepared unto glory?"

Then go on to Romans 11:7—"What then? Israel has not obtained that which he seeks for; but the Election has obtained it, and the rest were blinded." In the 5th verse of the same Chapter, we read—"Even so then at this present time also there is a remnant according to the Election of Grace." You, no doubt, all remember the passage in 1 Corinthians 1:26-29—"For you see your calling, Brethren, how that not many wise men after the flesh, not many mighty, not many noble, are called: but God has chosen the foolish things of the world to confound the wise; and God has chosen the weak things of the world to confound the things which are mighty; and base things of the world, and things which are despised, has God chosen, yes, and things which are not, to bring to nothing things that are: that no flesh should glory in His Presence." Again, remember the passage in 1 Thessalonians 5:9—"God has not appointed us to wrath, but to obtain salvation by our Lord Jesus Christ," and then you have my text, which I think would be quite enough. But if you need any more, you can find them at your leisure if we have not quite removed your suspicions as to the Doctrine not being true.

I think, my Friends, this overwhelming mass of Scripture testimony must stagger those who dare to laugh at this Doctrine! What shall we say of those who have so often despised it and denied its Divinity? What shall we say to those who have railed at its justice and dared to defy God and call Him an Almighty tyrant, when they have heard of His having elected so many to eternal life? Can you, O Rejecter, cast it out of the Bible? Can you take the penknife of Jehudi and cut it out of the Word of God? Would you be like the women at the feet of Solomon and have the child cut in half that you might have your half? Is it not here in Scripture? And is it not your duty to bow before it and meekly acknowledge what you understand not—to receive it as the Truth even though you could not understand its meaning? I will not attempt to prove the justice of God in having thus elected some and left others. It is not for me to vindicate my Master! He will speak for Himself and He does so—"But, O man, who are you that replies against God? Shall the thing formed say to Him that formed it, Why have you made me thus? Has not the potter power over the clay, of the same lump to make one vessel unto honor and another unto dishonor?" Who is he that shall say unto his father, "What have you begotten?"...or unto his mother, "What have you brought forth?" "I am the Lord—I form the light and create darkness. I, the Lord, do all these things. Who are you that replies against God? Tremble and kiss His rod; bow down and submit to His scepter; impugn not His justice and arraign not His acts before your bar, O man!"

But there are some who say, "It is hard for God to choose some and leave others." Now, I will ask you one question. Are there any of you here this morning who wish to be holy, who wish to be regenerate, to leave off sin and walk in holiness? "Yes," someone says, "I do." Then God has elected you! But another says, "No. I don't want to be holy. I don't want to give up my lusts and my vices." Why should you grumble, then, that God has not elected *you*? For if you were elected you would not like it, according to your own confession! If God, this morning, had chosen you to holiness you say you would not care for it. Do you not acknowledge that you prefer drunkenness to sobriety, dishonesty to honesty? You love this world's pleasures better than religion—then why should you grumble that God has not chosen you to religion? If you love religion, He has chosen you to it! If you desire it, He has chosen you to it! If you do not, what right do you have to say that God ought to have given you what you do not wish for? Supposing I had in my hand something which you do not value, and I said I shall give it to such-and-such a person—you would have no right to grumble that I did not give it to you! You could not be so foolish as to grumble that the other has got what you do not care about! According to your own confession, many of you do not want religion—do not want a new heart and a right spirit—do not want the forgiveness of sins! You do not want sanctification. You do not want to be elected to these things—then why should you grumble? You count these things but as husks, so why should you complain of God who has given them to those whom He has chosen? If you believe them to be good and desire them, they are there for you! God gives liberally to all those who desire—but first of all, *He* makes them desire—otherwise they never would. If you love these things, He has elected you to them and you may have them. But if you do not, who are you that you should find fault with God when it is your own desperate will that keeps you from loving these things? Suppose a man in the street should say, "What a shame it is I cannot have a seat in the Chapel to hear what this man has to say." And suppose he says, "I hate the preacher—I can't bear his Doctrine—but still, it's a shame I have not a seat"? Would you expect a man to say so? No—you would at once say, "That man does not care for it. Why should he trouble himself about other people having what they value and he despises?" You do not like holiness, you do not like righteousness. If God has elected me to these things, has He hurt you by it? "Ah, but," some say, "I thought it meant that God elected some to Heaven and some to Hell." That is a very different matter from the Gospel Doctrine! He has elected men to holiness and to righteousness—and through that to Heaven. You must not say that He has elected these simply to Heaven and others only to Hell. He has elected you to holiness if you love *holiness*. If any of you love to be saved by Jesus Christ— Jesus Christ elected you to be saved! If any of you desire to have salvation, you are elected to have it—if you desire it sincerely and earnestly! But, if you don't desire it, why on earth would you be so preposterously foolish as to grumble because God gives that which you do not like to other people?

II. Thus I have tried to say something with regard to the Truth of the Doctrine of Election. And now, briefly, let me say that Election is ABSOLUTE, that is, it does not depend upon what we are. The text says, "God has from the beginning chosen us unto salvation." But our opponents say that God chooses people because they are good—that He chooses them on account of sundry works which they have done. Now, we ask in reply to this, what works are those on account of which God elects His people? Are they what we commonly call, "works of Law"?—works of obedience which the creature can render? If so, we reply to you—If men cannot be *justified* by the works of the Law, it seems to us pretty clear that they cannot be *elected* by the works of the Law! If they cannot be justified by their good deeds, they cannot be saved by them. Then the decree of Election could not have been formed upon good works. "But," say others, "God elected them on the foresight of their faith." Now God *gives* faith, therefore He could not have elected them on *account* of faith which He foresaw. There shall be 20 beggars in the street and I determine to give one of them a shilling. Will anyone say that I determined to give that one a shilling—that I elected him to have the shilling—because I foresaw that he would have it? That would be talking nonsense! In like manner, to say that God elected men because He foresaw they would have faith—which is salvation in the germ—would be too absurd for us to listen to for a moment! Faith is the gift of God. Every virtue comes from Him. Therefore it cannot have caused Him to elect men, because it is His gift! Election, we are sure, is absolute and altogether apart from the virtues which the saints have afterwards. What if a saint should be as holy and devout as Paul? What if he should be as bold as Peter, or as loving as John? Still, he could claim nothing but what he received from his Maker! I never knew a saint yet, of any denomination, who thought that God saved him because He foresaw that he would have these virtues and merits. Now, my Brothers and Sisters, the best jewels that the saint ever wears, if they are jewels of our own fashioning, are not of the first water! There is something of earth mixed with them. The highest Grace we ever possess has something of earthliness about it. We feel this when we are most refined, when we are most sanctified and our language must always be—

"I the chief of sinners am;
Jesus died for me."

Our only hope, our only plea, still hangs on Grace as exhibited in the Person of Jesus Christ. And I am sure we must utterly reject and disregard all thought that our Graces, which are gifts of our Lord, which are His right-hand planting, could have ever caused His love. And we always must sing—

"What was there in us that could merit
esteem
Or give the Creator delight?
It was even so, Father, we always must
sing,
Because it seemed good in Your sight"

"He will have mercy on whom He will have mercy." He saves because He will save. And if you ask me why He saves me, I can only say because He would do it. Is there anything in me that should recommend me to God? No. I lay aside everything. I had nothing to recommend me. When God saved me, I was the most abject, lost and ruined of the race. I lay before Him as an infant in my blood. Verily, I had no power to help myself. O how wretched did I feel and know myself to be! If you had something to recommend you to God, I never had. I will be content to be saved by Grace, unalloyed, pure Grace. I can boast of no merits. If you can do so, still I cannot. I must sing—

"Free Grace alone from the first to the last Has won my affection and held my soul fast."

III. Then, thirdly, this Election is ETERNAL. "God has from the beginning chosen you unto eternal life." Can any man tell me when the beginning was? Years ago we thought the beginning of this world was when Adam came upon it. But we have discovered that thousands of years before that, God was preparing chaotic matter to make it a fit abode for man, putting races of creatures upon it who might die and leave behind the marks of His handiwork and marvelous skill before He tried His hand on man. But that was not the beginning, for Revelation points us to a period long before this world was fashioned—to the

days when the morning stars were begotten—
when, like drops of dew from the fingers of the
morning, stars and constellations fell trickling
from the hand of God. When, by His own lips,
He launched forth ponderous orbs. When with
His own hands He sent comets, like
thunderbolts, wandering through the sky to
find, one day, their proper sphere. We go back
to years gone by, when worlds were made and
systems fashioned, but we have not even
approached the beginning! Until we go to the
time when all the universe slept in the mind of
God as yet unborn—until we enter the eternity
where God the Creator lived alone, everything
sleeping within Him, all creation resting in His
mighty gigantic thought—we have not guessed
the beginning. We may go back, back, back,
ages upon ages. We may go back, if we might
use such strange words, whole eternities and
yet never arrive at the beginning! Our wings
might be tired, our imagination would die
away. Could it outstrip the lightning flashing
in majesty, power and rapidity, it would soon
weary itself before it could get to the beginning!
But God from the *beginning* chose His people
when the unnavigated ether was yet unfanned
by the wing of a single angel, when space was
shoreless, or else unborn, when universal
silence reigned and not a voice or whisper
shocked the solemnity of silence, when there

was no being and no motion, no time and nothing but God Himself, alone in His eternity—when without the song of an angel, without the attendance of even the cherubim—long before the living creatures were born, or the wheels of the chariot of Jehovah were fashioned—even then, "in the beginning was the Word," and in the beginning God's people were one with the Word and "in the beginning He chose them unto eternal life." Our Election, then, is eternal. I will not stop to prove it. I only just run over these thoughts for the benefit of young beginners, that they may understand what we mean by eternal, absolute Election.

IV. And, next, the Election is PERSONAL. Here again, our opponents have tried to overthrow Election by telling us that it is an Election of *nations*—and not of people. But here the Apostle says, "God has from the beginning chosen *you*." It is the most miserable shift on earth to make out that God has not chosen persons, but nations, because the very same objection that lies against the choice of persons lies against the choice of a nation! If it were not just to choose a *person* it would be far more unjust to choose a nation, since nations are but the union of multitudes of persons! To choose a nation seems to be a more gigantic crime—if Election is a crime—than to choose one person. Surely to choose ten thousand would be reckoned to be worse than choosing one—to distinguish a whole nation from the rest of mankind seems to be a greater extravaganza in the acts of Divine Sovereignty than the Election of one poor mortal and leaving out another. But what are nations but men? What are whole peoples but combinations of different units? A nation is made up of that individual, and that, and that. And if you tell me that God chose the Jews, I say, then, He chose that Jew and that Jew and that Jew. And if you say He chooses Britain, then I say He chooses that British person and that British person and that British person. So that it is the same thing, after all. Election, then, is personal—it must be so! Everyone who reads this text and others like it, will see that Scripture continually speaks of God's people one by one and speaks of them as having been the special subjects of Election—

"Sons we are through God's Election,
Who in Jesus Christ believe;
By eternal destination
Sovereign Grace we here receive."

We know it is personal Election.

V. The other thought is—for my time flies too swiftly to enable me to dwell at length upon these points—that Election produces GOOD RESULTS. "He has from the beginning chosen you unto sanctification of the Spirit and belief of the Truth." How many men mistake the Doctrine of Election altogether! And how my soul burns and boils at the recollection of the terrible evils that have accrued from the spoiling and the wresting of that glorious portion of God's glorious Truth! How many are there who have said to themselves, "I am elect," and have sat down in sloth and worse than that! They have said, "I am the elect of God," and with both hands they have done wickedness. They have swiftly run to every unclean thing because they have said, "I am the chosen child of God, irrespective of my works—therefore I may live as I like and do what I like." O, Beloved! Let me solemnly warn every one of you not to carry the Truth of God too far—or, rather not to turn the Truth of God into error, for we cannot carry it too far! We may overstep the Truth—we can make that which was meant to be sweet for our comfort a terrible mixture for our destruction. I tell you there have been thousands of men who have been ruined by misunderstanding Election— who have said, "God has elected me to Heaven and to eternal life"—but they have forgotten that it is written, God has elected them, "through sanctification of the Spirit and belief of the Truth." This is God's Election—Election to *sanctification* and to *faith.* God chooses His people to be holy and to be Believers! How many of you here, then, are Believers? How many of my congregation can put their hands upon their hearts and say, "I trust in God that I am sanctified"? Is there one of you who says, "I am elect"?

One of you says, "I trust I am elect"—but I jog your memory about some vicious act that you committed during the last six days. Another of you says, "I am elect"—but I would look you in the face and say, "*Elect?* You are a most cursed hypocrite and that is all you are!" Others would say, "I am elect"—but I would remind them that they neglect the Mercy Seat and do not pray. Oh, Beloved, never think you are elect unless you are *holy*. You may come to Christ as a sinner but you may not come to Christ as an elect person until you can see your holiness! Do not misconstrue what I say—do not say, "I am elect," and yet think you can be living in sin! That is impossible. The elect of God are holy. They are not pure, they are not perfect, they are not spotless—but taking their life as a whole, they are holy persons. They are marked and distinct from others—and no man has a right to conclude himself elect except in his holiness. He may be elect and yet lying in darkness, but he has no right to believe it. No one can say it, if there is no evidence of it. The man may live one day, but he is dead at present. If you are walking in the fear of God, trying to please Him and to obey His Commandments, doubt not that your name has been written in the Lamb's Book of Life from before the foundation of the world!

And, lest this should be too high for you, note the other mark of Election, which is faith— belief of the Truth of God. Whoever believes God's Truth and believes on Jesus Christ, is elect. I frequently meet with poor souls who are fretting and worrying themselves about this thought—"What if I should not be elect!" "Oh, Sir," they say, "I know I put my trust in Jesus. I know I believe in His name and trust in His blood. But what if I should not be elect?" Poor dear creature! You do not know much about the Gospel or you would never talk so, for *he that believes is elect.* Those who are elect are elect unto sanctification and unto faith. If you have faith, you are one of God's elect! You may know it and ought to know it, for it is an absolute certainty! If you, as a sinner, look to Jesus Christ this morning and say—

"Nothing in my hands I bring,
Simply to Your Cross I cling,"
you are elect! I am not afraid of Election frightening poor saints or sinners. There are many Divines who tell the inquirer, "Election has nothing to do with you." That is very bad,

because the poor soul is not to be silenced like that. If you could silence him so, it might be well—but he will think of it, he can't help it. Say to him, then, if you believe on the Lord Jesus Christ, you are elect. If you will cast yourself on Jesus, you are elect. I tell you—the chief of sinners—this morning—I tell you in His name—if you will come to God without any works of your own, cast yourself on the blood and righteousness of Jesus Christ—if you will come now and trust in Him, you are elect—you were loved of God from before the foundation of the world, for you could not do that unless God had given you the power and had chosen you to do it! Now you are safe and secure if you do but come and cast yourself on Jesus Christ and wish to be saved and to be loved by Him. But think not that any man will be saved without faith and without holiness. Do not conceive, my Hearers, that some decree passed in the dark ages of eternity will save your souls, unless you believe in Christ! Do not sit down and fancy that you are to be saved without faith and holiness! That is a most abominable and accursed heresy and has ruined thousands.

Lay not Election as a pillow for you to sleep on, or you may be ruined. God forbid that I should be sewing pillows under armholes that you may rest comfortably in your sins. Sinner, there is nothing in the Bible to lighten your sins! But if you are condemned, O Man!; if you are lost, O Woman!; you will not find in this Bible one drop to cool your tongue, or one Doctrine to lessen your guilt. Your damnation will be entirely your own fault and your sin will richly merit it—because you believe you are not condemned. "You believe not because you are not of My sheep. You will not come to Me that you might have life." Do not fancy that Election excuses sin—do not dream of it—do not rock yourself in sweet complacency in the thought of your irresponsibility! You are responsible. We must give you both things. We must have Divine Sovereignty and we must have man's responsibility. We must have Election, but we must ply your hearts—we must send God's Truth at you. We must speak to you and remind you of this, that while it is written, "In Me is your help," yet it is also written, "O Israel, you have destroyed yourself."

VI. Now, lastly, what are the true and legitimate tendencies of right conceptions concerning the Doctrine of Election? First, I will tell you what the Doctrine of Election will make saints do under the blessing of God. And, secondly what it will do for sinners if God blesses it to them.

First, I think Election, to a saint, is one of the most *stripping* Doctrines in all the world—to take away all trust in the flesh or all reliance upon anything except Jesus Christ. How often do we wrap ourselves up in our own righteousness and array ourselves with the false pearls and gems of our own works and doings? We begin to say, "Now I shall be saved, because I have this and that evidence." Instead of that, it is naked faith that saves—that faith, and that alone, unites to the Lamb— irrespective of works, although it is productive of them. How often do we lean on some work other than that of our own Beloved Jesus and trust in some might other than that which comes from on High? Now if we would have this might taken from us, we must consider Election. Pause, my Soul, and consider this. God loved you before you had a being! He loved you when you were dead in trespasses and sins and sent His Son to die for you! He purchased you with His precious blood before you could say His name! Can you, then, be *proud*?

I know nothing, nothing again, that is more *humbling* for us than this Doctrine of Election. I have sometimes fallen prostrate before it when endeavoring to understand it. I have stretched my wings and, eagle-like, I have soared towards the sun. Steady has been my eye and true my wing for a season. But, when I came near it and the one thought possessed me—"God has from the beginning chosen you unto salvation," I was lost in its luster! I was staggered with the mighty thought—and from the dizzy elevation down came my soul, prostrate and broken, saying, "Lord, I am nothing, I am less than nothing! Why me? Why me?"

Friends, if you want to be humbled, study Election, for it will make you humble under the influence of God's Spirit. He who is proud of his election is not elect—and he who is humbled under a sense of it may believe that he is. He has every reason to believe that he is, for it is one of the most blessed effects of Election—that it helps us to humble ourselves before God.

Once again—Election in the Christian should make him very *fearless* and very *bold*. No man will be so bold as he who believes that he is elect of God. What cares he for man if he is chosen of his Maker? What will he care for the pitiful chirpings of some tiny sparrows when he knows that he is an eagle of a royal race? Will he care when the beggar points at him when the blood royal of heaven runs in his veins? Will he fear if all the world stand against him? If earth is all in arms abroad, he dwells in perfect peace—for he is in the secret place of the tabernacle of the Most High, in the great pavilion of the Almighty! "I am God's," he says, "I am distinct from other men. They are of an inferior race. Am I not noble? Am I not one of the aristocrats of Heaven? Is not my name written in God's Book?" Does he care for the world? No—like the lion that cares not for the barking of the dog, he smiles at all his enemies—and when they come too near him, he moves himself and dashes them to pieces. What cares he for them? He walks about them like a colossus—while little men walk under him and understand him not. His brow is made of iron, his heart is of flint—what does he care for man? No—if one universal hiss came up from the wide world, he would smile at it, for he would say—

> *"He that has made his refuge God,*
> *Shall find a most secure abode."*

I am one of His elect. I am chosen of God and precious—and though the world cast me out, I fear not. Ah, you time-serving professors, some of you will bend like the willows! There are few oaken-Christians nowadays that can stand the storm—and I will tell you the reason. It is because you do not believe yourselves to be elect! The man who knows he is elect will be too proud to sin—he will not humble himself to commit the acts of common people. The believer in God's Truth will say, "*I* compromise my principles? *I* change my Doctrines? *I* lay aside my views? *I* hide what I believe to be true? No! Since I know I am one of God's elect, in the very teeth of all men I shall speak God's Truth whatever man may say." Nothing makes a man so truly bold as to feel that he is God's elect! He shall not quiver, he shall not shake— who knows that God has chosen him!

Moreover, Election will make us *holy*. Nothing under the gracious influence of the Holy Spirit can make a Christian more holy than the thought that he is chosen! "Shall I sin," he says, "after God has chosen me? Shall I transgress after such love? Shall I go astray after so much lovingkindness and tender mercy? No, my God, since You have chosen me, I will love You. I will live to You—
> **Since You, the everlasting God,**
> **My Father have become.**

I will give myself to You to be Yours forever, by Election and by Redemption, casting myself on You and solemnly consecrating myself to Your service."

And now, lastly, to the ungodly. What says Election to you? First, you ungodly ones, I will excuse you for a moment. There are many of you who do not like Election and I cannot blame you for it, for I have heard those preach

Election who have sat down and said, "I have not one word to say to the sinner." Now, I say you *ought* to dislike such preaching as that, and I do not blame you for it! But I say, take courage, take hope, O you Sinner, that there is Election! So far from dispiriting and discouraging you, it is a very hopeful and joyous thing that there is an Election. What if I told you, perhaps, none can be saved, none are ordained to eternal life? Would you not tremble and fold your hands in hopelessness and say, "Then how can I be saved, since none are elect?" But, I say there is a multitude of elect, beyond all counting—a host that no mortal can number! Therefore, take heart, poor Sinner! Cast away your despondency—may you not be elect as well as any other?—for there is chosen an innumerable host! There is joy and comfort for you! Then, not only take heart, but go and try the Master! Remember, if you were not elect, you would lose nothing by it. What did the four lepers say? "Let us fall unto the host of the Syrians, for if we stay here, we must die, and if we go to them, we can but die." O Sinner! Come to the Throne of electing mercy! You may die where you are. Go to God—and, even supposing He should spurn you, suppose His uplifted hand should drive you away—a thing impossible—yet you will not lose anything! You will not be more damned for that. Besides, supposing you are damned, you would at least have the satisfaction of being able to lift up your eyes in Hell and say, "God, I asked mercy of You and You would not grant it. I sought it, but You did refuse it." That you shall never say, O Sinner! If you go to Him and ask Him, you shall receive—for He never has spurned one yet! Is not that hope for you? Though there is an allotted number, yet it is true that all who seek belong to that number! Go and seek—and if you should be the first one to go to Hell, tell the devils that you did perish thus—tell the demons that you are a castaway after having come as a guilty sinner to Jesus. I tell you it would disgrace the Eternal—with reverence to His name—and He would not allow such a thing! He is jealous of His honor and He could not allow a sinner to say that!

But ah, poor Soul! Do not think thus, that you can lose anything by coming! There is yet one more thought—do you love the thought of Election this morning? Are you willing to admit its justice? Do you say, "I feel that I am lost. I deserve it and if my brother is saved, I cannot murmur. If God destroys me, I deserve it, but if He saves the person sitting beside me, He has a right to do what He will with His own and I have lost nothing by it." Can you say that honestly from your heart? If so, then the

Doctrine of Election has had its right effect on your spirit and you are not far from the Kingdom of Heaven! You are brought where you ought to be, where the Spirit wants you to be—and being so this morning, depart in peace! God has forgiven your sins! You would not feel that if you were not pardoned—you would not feel that if the Spirit of God were not working in you! Rejoice, then, in this! Let your hope rest on the Cross of Christ. Think not on Election, but on Christ Jesus. Rest on Jesus—Jesus first, last, and without end!

L

Limited

Atonement

CHRIST'S PASTORAL PRAYER FOR HIS PEOPLE

A SERMON DELIVERED
ON LORD'S-DAY EVENING, SEPTEMBER 1,
1889.
By C. H. SPURGEON

AT THE METROPOLITAN TABERNACLE,
NEWINGTON,

*"I pray for them: I pray not for the world,
but for them which thou hast given me; for
they are thine.
And all mine are thine, and thine are mine;
and I am glorified in them."*
John 17:9-10

To begin with, I remark that our Lord Jesus
pleads for His own people. When He puts on
His priestly breastplate, it is for the tribes
whose names are there. When He presents the
atoning Sacrifice, it is for Israel whom God has
chosen, and He utters this great Truth of God,
which some regard as narrow, but which we
adore, "I pray for them: I pray not for the
world." The point to which I want to call
attention is this—the reason why Christ prays
not for the world, but for His people. He puts
it, "For they are Yours," as if they were all the

dearer to Him because they were the Father's—"I pray for them: I pray not for the world, but for them which You have given Me, for they are Yours." We might have half thought that Jesus would have said, "They are Mine and, therefore, I pray for them." It would have been true, but there would not have been the beauty of Truth about it which we have here. He loves us all the better and He prays for us all the more fervently because we are the *Father's*. Such is His love to His Father, that our being the Father's sheds upon us an extra halo of beauty! Because we belong to the Father, therefore does the Savior plead for us with all the greater earnestness at the Throne of the heavenly Grace.

But this leads us on to remember that our Lord had undertaken suretyship engagements on account of His people—He undertook to preserve the Father's gift—"Those that You gave Me, I have kept, and none of them is lost." He looked upon the sheep of His pasture as belonging to His Father and the Father had put them into His charge, saying to Him, "Of Your hand will I require them." As Jacob kept his uncle's flocks—by day the heat devoured him and at night the frost—but he was more careful over them because they were Laban's than if they had been his own. He was to give an account of all the sheep committed to him and he did so—and he lost none of Laban's sheep. His care over them was partly accounted for by the fact that they did not belong to himself, but belonged to his uncle, Laban.

Understand this twofold reason, then, for Christ's pastoral prayer for His people. He first prays for them because they belong to the Father and, therefore, have a peculiar value in His eyes. And next, because they belong to the Father, He is under suretyship engagements to deliver them all to the Father in that Last Great Day when the sheep shall pass under the rod of Him that counts them. Now you see where I am bringing you tonight. I am not going to preach at this time to the world any more than Christ, upon this occasion, prayed for the world. But I am going to preach to His own people as He, in this intercessory prayer, pleaded for them. I trust that they will all follow me, step by step, through this great theme, and I pray the Lord that, in these deep central Truths of the Gospel, we may find real refreshment for our souls tonight.

I. In calling your attention to my text, I want you to notice, first, THE INTENSITY OF THE SENSE OF PROPERTY WHICH CHRIST HAS IN HIS PEOPLE.

Here are *six words setting forth Christ's property in those who are saved*—"Them which You have given Me"—(that is one), "for they are Yours. And all Mine are Yours, and Yours are Mine; and I am glorified in them." There are certain persons so precious to Christ that they are marked all over with special tokens that they belong to Him, as I have known a man write his name in a book which he has greatly valued and then he has turned over some pages and written his name again, and, as we have sometimes known persons, when they have highly valued a thing, to put their mark, their seal, their stamp here, there and almost everywhere upon it! So, notice in my text how the Lord seems to have the seal in His hand and He stamps it all over His peculiar possession! "They are Yours. And all Mine are Yours, and Yours are Mine." It is all possessive pronouns, to show that God looks upon His people as His portion, His possession, His property. "They shall be Mine, says the Lord of Hosts, in that day when I make up My jewels." Every man has something or other which he values above the rest of his estate and here the Lord, by so often reiterating the words which signify possession, proves that He values His people above everything! Let us show that we appreciate this privilege of being set apart unto God and let us each one say to Him—

> *"Take my poor heart, and let it be*
> *Forever closed to all but Thee!*
> *Seal You my breast and let me wear*
> *That pledge of love forever there."*

I call your attention, next, to the fact that, while there are these six expressions here, *they are all applied to the Lord's own people.* "My," (that is, the saints), are Yours, (that is, the saints), are Mine, (that is, the saints). These broad arrows of the King of Kings are all stamped upon His people! While the marks of possession are numerous they are all set upon one object. What? Does not God care for anything else? I answer, "No." As compared with His own people, He cares for nothing else. "The Lord's portion is His people: Jacob is the lot of His inheritance." Has not God other things? Ah, what is there that He has *not*? The silver and the gold are His and the cattle on a thousand hills. All things are of God—of Him, and by Him, and through Him, and to Him are all things—yet He reckons them not in comparison with His people! You know how you, dearly Beloved, value your children much more than you do anything else. If there were a fire in your house tonight, and you could only carry one thing out of it, Mother, would you hesitate a moment as to what that one thing would be? You would carry your baby and let everything else be consumed in the flames! And it is so with God. He cares for His people beyond everything else. He is the Lord God of Israel, and in Israel He has set His name, and there He takes His delight. There does He rest in His love and over her does He rejoice with singing!

I want you to notice these different points, not because I can fully explain them all to you, but if I can only give you some of these great Truths to think about and to help you to communion with Christ tonight, I shall have done well. I want you to note, yet further, concerning these notes of possession, that *they occur in the private communion between the Father and the Son.* It is in our Lord's prayer, when He is in the inner sanctuary speaking with the Father, that we have these words, "All Mine are Yours, and Yours are Mine." It is not to you and to me that He is talking, now. The Son of God is speaking with the Father when They are in very near communion, One with the Other. Now, what does this say to me but that the Father and the Son greatly value Believers? What people talk about when they are alone—not what they say in the market, not what they talk of in the midst of the confused mob, but what they say when they are in private—that lays bare their heart! Here is the Son speaking to the Father, not about thrones and royalties, nor cherubim and seraphim, but about poor men and women—in those days mostly fishermen and peasant folk—who believed on Him!

They are talking about these people and the Son is taking His own solace with the Father in Their secret privacy by talking about these precious jewels, these dear ones that are Their peculiar treasure. You have not any notion how much God loves you! Dear Brother, dear Sister, you have never yet had half an idea, or the tithe of an idea, of how precious you are to Christ! You think because you are so imperfect and you fall so much below your own ideal, that, therefore, He does not love you much. You think that He cannot do so. Have you ever measured the depth of Christ's agony in Gethsemane and of His death on Calvary? If you have tried to do so, you will be quite sure that, apart from anything in you or about you, He loves you with a love that passes knowledge! Believe it. "But I do not love Him as I should," I think I hear you say. No, and you never will unless you first know His love to you. Believe it! Believe it to the highest degree, that He so loves you that when there is no one who can commune with Him but the Father, even *then* Their talk is about Their mutual estimate of you—how much They love you! "All Mine are Yours, and Yours are Mine."

Only one other thought under this head and I but put it before you and leave it with you, for I cannot expound it tonight. *All that Jesus says is about all His people,* for He says, "All Mine are Yours, and Yours are Mine." These high, secret talks are not about some few saints who have reached a "higher life," but about all of us who belong to Him! Jesus bears all of us on His heart and He speaks of us all to the Father—"All Mine are Yours." "That poor woman who could never serve her Lord except by patient endurance, she is Mine," says Jesus. "She is Yours, great Father." "That poor girl, newly-converted, whose only spiritual life was spent upon a sickbed and then she exhaled to Heaven, like a dewdrop of the morning, she is Mine, and she is Yours." "That poor child who often stumbles, who never brought much credit to the sacred name, He is Mine and He is Yours." "All Mine are Yours." I seem as if I heard a silver bell ringing out! The very tones of the words are like the music from the harps of angels! "My—Yours. Yours—Mine." May such sweet risings and fallings of heavenly melodies charm all our ears!

I think that I have said enough to show you the intensity of the sense of property which

Christ has in His people—"All Mine are Yours, and Yours are Mine."

II. The next head of my discourse is THE INTENSITY OF UNITED INTEREST BETWEEN THE FATHER AND THE SON CONCERNING BELIEVERS.

First, let me say that *Jesus loves us because we belong to the Father*. Turn that Truth of God over. "My Father has chosen them, My Father loves them. Therefore," says Jesus, "I love them and I lay down My life for them, and I will take My life again for them, and live throughout eternity for them. They are dear to Me because they are dear to My Father." Have you not often loved another person for the sake of a third one upon whom all your heart was set? There is an old proverb and I cannot help quoting it just now. It is, "Love me, love my dog." It is as if the Lord Jesus so loved the Father that even such poor dogs as we are get loved by Him for His Father's sake! To the eyes of Jesus we are radiant with beauty because God has loved us.

Now turn that thought round the other way, *the Father loves us because we belong to Christ*. At first, the Father's love in election was Sovereign and self-contained, but now, since He has given us over to Christ, He takes a greater delight in us. "They are My Son's sheep," He says, "He bought them with His blood." Better still—"That is My Son's spouse," He says. "That is My Son's bride. I love her for His sake." There was that first love which came fresh from the Father's heart, but now, through this one channel of love to Jesus, the Father pours a double flood of love on us for His dear Son's sake. He sees the blood of Jesus sprinkled on us. He remembers the token and, for the sake of His beloved Son, He prizes us beyond all price! Jesus loves us because we belong to the Father—and the Father loves us because we belong to Jesus!

Now come still closer to the central thought of the text, All Mine are Yours." *All who are the Son's are the Father's.* Do we belong to Jesus? Then we belong to the Father! Have I been washed in the precious blood? Can I sing, tonight—

> **"The dying thief rejoiced to see**
> **That fountain in his day!**
> **And there have I, though vile as he,**
> **Washed all my sins away"**?

Then, by redemption I belong to Christ! But, at the same time, I may be sure that I belong to the Father—"All Mine are Yours." Are you trusting in Christ? Then you are one of God's elect! That high and deep mystery of predestination need trouble no man's heart if he is a believer in Christ. If you believe in Christ, Christ has redeemed you and the Father chose you from before the foundation of the world! You may rest happily in that firm belief, "All Mine are Yours." How often have I met with people puzzling themselves about election! They want to know if they are elect. No man can come to the Father but by Christ—no man can come to election except through redemption! If you have come to Christ and are His redeemed, it is certain beyond all doubt that you were chosen of God and are the Father's elect. "All Mine are Yours."

So, if I am bought by Christ's precious blood, I am not to sit down and say how grateful I am to Christ as though He were apart from the Father and more loving and more tender than the Father. No, no! I belong to the Father if I belong to Christ—and I have for the Father the same gratitude, the same love, and I would render the same service as to Jesus, for Jesus puts it, "All Mine are Yours."

If tonight I am a servant of Christ; if, because He bought me I try to serve Him, then I am also a servant of the Father if I am a servant of the Son. "All Mine, whatever position they occupy, belong to You, great Father," and they have all the privileges which come to those who belong to the Father. I hope that I do not weary you. I cannot make these things entertaining to the careless—I do not try to do so. But you who love my Lord and His Truth ought to rejoice to think that, in being the property of Christ, you are assured that you are the property of the Father! "All Mine are Yours."—

"With Christ our Lord we share our part
In the affections of His heart.
Nor shall our souls be removed
Till He forgets His First-Beloved."

But now you have to look at the other part of it—"and Yours are Mine." *All who are the Father's are the Son's.* If you belong to the Father, you belong to the Son. If you are elect, and so the Father's, you are redeemed, and so the Son's. If you are adopted, and so the Father's, you are justified in Christ and so you are the Son's. If you are regenerated, and so are begotten of the Father, your life is still dependent upon the Son. Remember that while one Biblical figure sets us forth as children who each have a life within himself, another equally valid figure represents us as branches of the Vine which die unless they continue united to the Stem. "All Yours are Mine." If you are the Father's, you must be Christ's. If your life is given you of the Father, it still depends entirely upon the Son.

What a wonderful mixture all this is! The Father and the Son are One and we are one with the Father and with the Son! A mystic union is established between us and the Father by reason of our union with the Son and the Son's union with the Father. See to what a glorious height our humanity has risen through Christ! By the Grace of God, you who were like stones in the brook are made sons of God! Lifted out of your dead materialism, you are elevated into a spiritual life and you are united to God! You have not any idea of what God has already done for you and truly, it does not yet appear what you shall be. A Christian man is the noblest work of God! God has here reached the fullness of His power and His Grace in making us to be one with His own dear Son, and so bringing us into union and communion with Himself. Oh, if the words that I speak could convey to you the fullness of their own meaning, you might spring to your feet, electrified with holy joy to think of this— that we should be Christ's and the Father's— and that we should be thought worthy to be the object of intricate transactions and inter-communions of the dearest kind between the Father and the Son! We, even we, who are but dust and ashes at our very best, are favored as angels never were! Therefore let all praise be ascribed to Sovereign Grace!

III. And now I shall only detain you a few minutes longer while I speak upon the third part of our subject, that is, THE GLORY OF CHRIST. "And I am glorified in them." I must confess that while the former part of my subject was very deep, this third part seems to me to be still deeper—"I am glorified in them."

If Christ had said, "I will glorify them," I could have understood it. If He had said, "I am pleased with them," I might have set it down to His great kindness to them. But when He says, "I am glorified in them," it is very amazing. The sun can be reflected, but you need proper objects to act as reflectors—and the brighter they are, the better will they reflect. You and I do not seem to have the power of reflecting Christ's Glory. We break up the glorious rays that shine upon us. We spoil; we ruin so much of the good that falls upon us. Yet Christ says that He is glorified in us! Take these words home, dear Friend, to yourself. What if the Lord Jesus met you tonight and, as you went out of the Tabernacle, said to you, "You are Mine. You are My Father's and I am glorified in you."? I dare not say that it would be a proud moment for you, but I dare say that there would be more in it to make you feel exalted for Him to say, "I am glorified in you," than if you could have all the honors that all the kings can put upon all men in the world! I think that

I could say, "Lord, now let Your servant depart in peace, according to Your Word," if He would but say to me, "I am glorified in your ministry." I hope that He is. I believe that He is, but, oh, for an assuring word, if not spoken to us personally, yet spoken to His Father about us, as in our text, "I am glorified in them"!

How can this be? Well, it is a very wide subject. Christ is glorified in His people in many ways. *He is glorified by saving such sinners*—taking these people, so sinful, so lost, so unworthy. When the Lord lays hold upon a drunk, a thief, an adulterer; when He arrests one who has been guilty of blasphemy, whose very heart is reeking with evil thoughts; when He picks up the far-off one, the abandoned, the dissolute, the fallen, as He often does, and when He says, "These shall be Mine. I will wash these in My blood. I will use these to speak My Word." Oh, then He is glorified in them! Read the lives of many great sinners who have afterwards become great saints and you will see how they have tried to glorify Him, not only she who washed His feet with her tears, but many another like her. Oh, how they have loved to praise Him! Eyes have wept tears, lips have spoken words—but hearts have felt what neither eyes nor lips could speak—of adoring gratitude to Him. "I am glorified in them." Great sinners, Christ is glorified in you! Some of you Pharisees, if you were to be converted, would not bring Christ such Glory as He gets through saving publicans and harlots! Even if you struggled into Heaven, it would be with very little music for Him on the road, certainly no tears and no ointment for His feet, and no wiping them with the hairs of your head! You are too respectable ever to do that. But when He saves great sinners, He can truly say, "I am glorified in them," and each of them can sing—

"It passes praises, that dear love of Yours,
My Jesus, Savior: yet this heart of mine
Would sing that love, so full, so rich, so
free,
Which brings a rebel sinner, such as me,
Near unto God."

And *Christ is glorified by the perseverance which He shows in the matter of their salvation.* See how He begins to save and the man resists. He follows up His kind endeavor and the man rebels. He hunts him, pursues him, dogs his footsteps. He will have the man, but the man will not have Him! But the Lord, without violating the free will of man, which He never does, yet at length brings the one who was most unwilling to lie at His feet and he that hated most begins to love! And he that was most stout-hearted bows his knees in lowliest humility. It is amazing how persevering the Lord is in the salvation of a sinner—yes, and in the salvation of His own, for you would have broken loose long ago if your great Shepherd had not penned you up within the fold! Many of you would have started aside and have lost yourselves if it had not been for constraints of Sovereign Grace which have kept you to this day and will not let you go! Christ is glorified in you. Oh, when you once get to Heaven, when the angels know all that you were and all that you tried to be; when the whole story of Almighty, Infinite Grace is told, as it will be told, then will Christ be glorified in you!

Beloved, *we actively glorify Christ when we display Christian Graces.* You who are loving, forgiving, tenderhearted, gentle, meek, self-sacrificing—you glorify Him—He is glorified in you; you who are upright and who will not be moved from your integrity; you who can despise the sinner's gold and will not sell your conscience for it; you who are bold and brave for Christ; you who can bear and suffer for His name's sake—all your Graces come from Him! As all the flowers are bred and begotten of the sun, so all that is in you that is good comes from Christ, the Sun of Righteousness! And therefore He is glorified in you.

But, Beloved, God's people have glorified
Christ in many other ways. *When they make
Him the object of all their trust, they glorify Him*;
when they say, "Though I am the chief of
sinners I trust Him. Though my mind is dark
and though my temptations abound, I believe
that He can save to the uttermost, I trust
Him." Christ is more glorified by a sinner's
humble faith than by a seraph's loudest song!
If you believe, you glorify Him. Child of God,
are you, tonight, very dark, dull and heavy? Do
you feel half dead spiritually? Come to your
Lord's feet and kiss them—and believe that He
can save—no, that He has saved you, even
you, and thus you will glorify His holy name.
"Oh," said a Believer, the other day, "I know
whom I have believed. Christ is mine!" "Ah,"
said another," that is *presumption*." Beloved, it
is nothing of the kind! It is not presumption for
a child to acknowledge his own father. It might
be pride for him to be ashamed of his father—
it is certainly great alienation from his father if
he is ashamed to acknowledge him. "I know
whom I have believed." Happy state of heart, to
be absolutely sure that you are resting upon
Christ, that He is your Savior, that you believe
in Him, for Jesus said, "He that believes on Me
has everlasting life." I believe on Him and I
have everlasting life! "He that believes on Him
is not condemned." I believe on Him and I am

not condemned! Make sure work of this, not only by signs and evidences, but do even better—make the one sign and the one evidence to be this—"Jesus Christ came into the world to save sinners. I, a sinner, accept His great Sacrifice and I am saved."

Especially, I think that *God's people glorify Christ by a cheerful conversation.* If you go about moaning and mourning, pining and complaining, you bring no honor to His name. But if, when you fast, you appear not unto men to fast; if you can wear a cheerful countenance even when your heart is heavy, and if, above all, you can rally your spirit out of its depths and begin to bless God when the cupboard is empty, and friends are few, then you will, indeed, glorify Christ!

Many are the ways in which this good work may be done—let us try to do it. "I am glorified in them," says Christ. That is, *by their bold confession of Christ.* Do I address myself to any here who love Christ, but who have never acknowledged it? Come out and come out very soon! He deserves to have all the glory that you can give Him. If He has healed you, be not like the nine who forgot that Christ had healed their leprosy. Come and praise the name of the great Healer and let others know what Christ can do! I am afraid that there are a great many here tonight who hope that they are Christians, but they have never said so. What are you ashamed of? Are you ashamed of your Lord? I am afraid that you do not, after all, love Him! Now, at this time, at this particular crisis in the history of the Church and the world, if we do not publicly take sides with Christ, we shall really be against Him! The time has now come when we cannot afford to have go-betweens. You must be for Him or for His enemies. Tonight He asks you if you are really His to say it! Come forward, unite yourself with His people and let it be seen by your life and conversation that you belong to Christ! If not, how can it be true, "I am glorified in them"? Is Christ glorified in a non-confessing people, a people that hope to go slinking into Heaven by the by-roads or across the fields, but dare not come into the King's Highway and travel with the King's subjects, and confess that they belong to Him?

Lastly, I think that *Christ is glorified in His people by their efforts to extend His Kingdom.* What efforts are you making? There is a great deal of force in a Church like this, but I am afraid that there is a great deal of wasted steam, wasted power, here. The tendency so often is to leave everything to be done by the minister, or else by one or two leading people. But I pray you, Beloved, if you are Christ's, and if you belong to the Father, if, unworthy though you are, you are claimed with a double ownership by the Father and the Son, try to be of use to Them! Let it be seen by your winning others to Christ that He is glorified in you! I believe that, by diligent attendance to even the smallest Sunday school class, Christ is glorified in you; by that private conversation in your own room; by that letter which you dropped into the post with many a prayer; by *anything* that you have done with a pure motive, trusting in God in order to glorify Christ, He is glorified in you!

Do not mistake my meaning with regard to serving the Lord. I think it exceedingly wrong when I hear exhortations made to young people, "Quit your service as domestics and come out into spiritual work. Business men, leave your shops. Workmen, give up your trades. You cannot serve Christ in that calling, come away from it altogether." I beg to say that *nothing* will be more pestilent than such advice as that! There are men called by the Grace of God to separate themselves from every earthly occupation and they have special gifts for the work of the ministry, but to ever imagine that the bulk of Christian people cannot serve God in their daily calling is to think altogether contrary to the mind of the Spirit of God! If you are a servant, remain a servant! If you are a waiter, go on with your waiting! If you are a tradesman, go on with your trade! Let every man abide in the calling wherein he is called, unless there is in him some special call from God to devote himself to the ministry. Go on with your employment, dear Christian people, and do not imagine that you are to turn into hermits, or monks, or nuns! You would not glorify God if you did so!

Soldiers of Christ are to fight the battle out where they are. To quit the field and shut yourselves up would be to render it impossible that you should get the victory. The work of God is as holy and acceptable in domestic service, or in trade, as any service that can be rendered in the pulpit, or even by the foreign missionary! We thank God for the men specially called and set apart for His work, but we know that they could do nothing unless the salt of our holy faith should permeate the daily life of other Christians. You godly mothers— you are the glory of the Church of Christ! You hard working men and women who endure patiently, "as seeing Him who is invisible," are the crown and glory of the Church of God! You who do not shirk your daily labor, but stand manfully to it, obeying Christ in it, are proving what the Christian religion was meant to do! We can, if we are truly priests unto God, make our everyday garments into vestments, our meals into sacraments and our houses into temples for God's worship! Our very beds will be within the veil, and our inmost thoughts will be as a sweet incense perpetually smoking up to the Most High. Dream not that there is *anything* about any honest calling that degrades a man, or hinders him in glorifying God! But sanctify it all till the bells upon the horses shall ring out, "Holiness to the Lord," and the pots in your houses shall be as holy as the vessels of the sanctuary!

Now, I want that we should so come to the Communion Table, that even here Christ may be glorified in us. Ah, you may sit at the Lord's Table wearing a fine dress or a diamond ring and you may think that you are somebody of importance, but you are not! Ah, you may come to the Lord's Table and say, "Here is an experienced Christian man who knows a thing or two." You are not glorifying Christ that way—you are only a nobody! But if you come saying, "Lord, I am hungry, You can feed me"— that is glorifying Him! If you come saying, "Lord, I have no merit and no worthiness. I come because You have died for me and I trust You"—you are glorifying Him! He glorifies Christ most who takes most *from* Him and who then gives most back *to* Him! Come, empty pitcher, come and be filled! And, when you are filled, pour all out at the dear feet of Him who filled you! Come, trembler, let Him touch you with His strengthening hands, and then go out and work—and use the strength which He has given you! I fear that I have not led you where I wanted to bring you—close to my Lord and to the Father—yet I have done my best. May the Lord forgive my feebleness and wandering, and yet bless you for His dear name's sake! Amen.

I

Irresistible Grace

PREDESTINATION AND CALLING

DELIVERED ON LORD'S DAY MORNING,
MARCH 6, 1859,
BY C. H. SPURGEON,

AT THE MUSIC HALL, ROYAL SURREY
GARDENS.

*"Moreover whom He did predestinate, them
He also called."*
Romans 8:30.

THE GREAT BOOK OF GOD'S DECREES is
fast closed against the curiosity of man. Vain
man would be wise; he would break the seven
seals thereof and read the mysteries of
eternity. But this cannot be! The time has not
yet come when the book shall be opened and
even then the seals shall not be broken by
mortal hand, but it shall be said, "The Lion of
the tribe of Judah has prevailed to open the
book and break the seven seals thereof."—

*Eternal Father, who shall look
Into Your secret will?
None but the Lamb shall take the book
And open every seal!*

None but He shall ever unroll that sacred
record and read it to the assembled world.
How, then, am I to know whether I am
predestinated by God unto eternal life or not?
It is a question in which my eternal interests

are involved—am I among that unhappy number who shall be left to live in sin and reap the due reward of their iniquity? Or do I belong to that goodly company who, albeit that they have sinned, shall nevertheless be washed in the blood of Christ and shall in white robes walk the golden streets of Heaven? Until this question is answered, my heart cannot rest, for I am intensely anxious about it. My eternal destiny infinitely more concerns me than all the affairs of time! Tell me, oh tell me, if you know, Seers and Prophets, is my name recorded in that Book of Life? Am I one of those who are ordained unto eternal life, or am I to be left to follow my own lusts and passions and to destroy my own soul? Oh, my Hearer, there is an answer to your inquiry! The book cannot be opened, but God Himself has published many a page thereof. He has not published the page whereon the actual names of the redeemed are written, but that page of the sacred decree whereon their *character* is recorded is published in His Word and shall be proclaimed to you this day! The sacred record of God's hand is this day published everywhere under Heaven and he who has an ear let him hear what the Spirit says to him! O my Hearer, by your name I know you not and by your name God's Word does not declare you, but by your *character* you may read your name! And if you have been a partaker of the calling which is mentioned in the text, then may you conclude beyond a doubt that you are among the predestinated—"For whom He did predestinate, them He also called." And if you are called, it follows as a natural inference you are predestinated!

Now, in considering this solemn subject, let me remark that there are two kinds of callings mentioned in the Word of God. The first is the *general* or *universal* call, which in the Gospel is sincerely given to everyone who hears the Word. The duty of the minister is to call souls to Christ; he is to make no distinction whatever—"Go you into all the world and preach the Gospel to every creature." The trumpet of the Gospel sounds aloud to every man in our congregations—"Ho, everyone who thirsts, come you to the waters and he that has no money, come you, buy and eat; yes, come, buy wine and milk without money and without price." "Unto you, O men, I call; and My voice is to the sons of man" (Proverbs 8:4). This call is sincere on God's part. But man by nature is so opposed to God that this call is never *effectual,* for man disregards it; turns his back upon it and goes his way caring for none of these things. But mark, although this call is rejected, man is without excuse in the rejection! The universal call has in it such authority that the man who will not obey it shall be without excuse in the Day of Judgment. When you are commanded to believe and repent—when you are exhorted to flee from the wrath to come—the sin lies on your own head if you despise the exhortation and reject the commandment! And this solemn text drops an awful warning—"How shall you escape if you neglect so great salvation?" But I repeat it—this universal call is rejected by man! It is a call, but it is not attended with the Divine force and energy of the Holy Spirit in such a degree as to make it an unconquerable call. Consequently, men perish even though they have the universal call of the Gospel ringing in their ears! The bell of God's House rings every day. Sinners hear it, but they put their fingers in their ears and go their way— some to his farm and another to his merchandise. Though they are bid and are called to the wedding (Luke 14:16-18), yet they will not come; and by not coming they incur God's wrath and He declares of such—"None of those men which were bid shall taste of My supper" (Luke 14:24). The call of our text is of a different kind. It is not a *universal* call, it is a special, particular, personal, discriminating, efficacious, call! This call is sent to the predestinated and only to them. They, by Divine Grace hear the call, obey it and receive it! These are they who can now say, "Draw us and we will run after You."

In preaching of this call this morning, I shall divide my sermon into three brief parts. First, I shall give *illustrations of the call.* Second, we shall come to *examine whether we have been called.* And then third, *what delightful consequences flow from there.* Illustration, examination, and consolation.

I. First, then, for ILLUSTRATION. In illustrating the effectual call of Grace which is given to the predestinated ones, I must first use the picture of Lazarus. See that stone rolled at the mouth of the sepulcher? Much need is there for the stone that it should be well secured, for within the sepulcher there is a putrid corpse. The sister of that corrupt body stands at the side of the tomb and she says, "Lord, by this time he stinks, for he has been dead four days." This is the voice of reason and of nature. Martha is correct. But by Martha's side there stands a Man who, despite all His lowliness, is very God of very God! "Roll away the stone," He said. And it was done. And now, listen to Him! He cries, "Lazarus, come forth!" That cry is directed to a mass of putridity; to a body that has been dead four days and in which the worms have already held carnival. But, strange to say, from that tomb there comes a living man! That mass of corruption has been quickened into life and out he comes, wrapped about with grave clothes and having a napkin about his head. "Loose him and let him go," said the Redeemer. And then Lazarus walks in all the liberty of life!

The *effectual* call of Grace is precisely similar. The sinner is dead in sin. He is not only in sin but *dead* in sin, without any power whatever to give to himself the life of Grace. No, he is not only dead, but he is corrupt! His lusts, like the worms, have crept into him. A foul stench rises up into the nostrils of Justice, God abhors him and Justice cries, "Bury the dead out of my sight, cast it into the fire; let it be consumed." Sovereign Mercy comes and there lies this unconscious, lifeless mass of sin. Sovereign Grace cries, either by the minister, or else directly without any agency, by the Spirit of God, "come forth!" and that man lives! Does he contribute anything to his new life? Not he— his life is given solely by God! He was dead, absolutely dead—rotten in his sin. The life is given when the call comes and, in obedience to the call, the sinner comes forth from the grave of his lust and begins to live a new life—even the life eternal which Christ gives to His sheep.

"Well," cries one, "but what are the words which Christ uses when He calls a sinner from death?" Why the Lord may use *any* words! It was not long ago there came into this hall a man who was without God and without Christ and the simple reading of the hymn—

"Jesus, Lover of my soul,"

was the means of his quickening! He said within himself, "Does Jesus love *me*? Then I must love Him," and he was quickened in that same hour! The words which Jesus uses are various in different cases. I trust that even while I am speaking this morning, Christ may speak within me and some word that may fall from my lips, unpremeditated and almost without design, shall be sent of God as a message of life unto some dead and corrupt heart! May, by His Grace, some man or woman who has lived in sin up to now, shall now live to righteousness and live to Christ! That is the first illustration I will give you of what is meant by effectual calling. It finds the sinner dead; it gives him life and he obeys the call of life and lives.

But let us consider a second phase of it. You will remember while the sinner is dead in sin, he is alive enough as far as any opposition to God may be concerned. He is powerless to *obey*, but he is mighty enough to *resist* the call of Divine Grace! I may illustrate it in the case of Saul of Tarsus—this proud Pharisee abhors the Lord Jesus Christ—he has seized upon every follower of Jesus who comes within his grasp! With the avidity of a miser who hunts after gold he has hauled men and women to prison! He has hunted after the precious life of Christ's disciple and having exhausted his prey in Jerusalem, he seeks letters and goes off to Damascus upon the same bloody errand. Speak to him on the road; send out the Apostle Peter to him; let Peter say, "Saul, why do you oppose Christ? The time shall come when you shall yet be His disciple." Paul would turn round and laugh him to scorn—Get out of here, fisherman! Get out of here —*I*, a disciple of that imposter Jesus of Nazareth? Look here, this is my confession of faith—here will I haul your brothers and your sisters to prison and beat them in the synagogue and compel them to blaspheme and even hunt them to death; for my breath is threatening and my heart is as fire against Christ." Such a scene did not occur, but had there been any remonstrance given by men, you may easily conceive that such would have been Saul's answer. But Christ determined that He *would* call the man before the foundation of the world! Oh, what an enterprise! Stop HIM? Why he is going fast onward in his mad career! But lo, a light shines round about him and he falls to the ground and he hears a voice crying, "Saul, Saul, why do you persecute Me? It is hard for you to kick against the pricks." Saul's eyes are filled with tears and then again with scales of darkness and he cries, "Who are You?" And a voice calls, "I am Jesus, whom you persecute." It is not many minutes before he begins to feel his sin in having persecuted Jesus, nor many hours before he receives the assurance of his pardon and not many days before he who persecuted Christ stands up to preach with vehemence and eloquence unparalleled, the very cause which he once trod beneath his feet!

See what effectual calling can do? If God should choose this morning to call the hardest-hearted wretch within hearing of the Gospel, he would obey! Let God call—a man may resist, but he cannot resist effectually! Down you shall come, Sinner, if God cries *down*! There is no standing when He would have you fall. And every man who is saved is always saved by an overcoming call which he cannot withstand. He may resist it for a time, but he cannot resist so as to overcome it—he must give way—he must yield when God speaks! If He says, "Let there be light," the impenetrable darkness gives way to light! If He says, "Let there be Grace," unutterable sin gives way and the hardest-hearted sinner melts before the fire of *effectual calling*!

I have thus illustrated the call in two ways—by the state of the sinner in his sin and by the Omnipotence which overwhelms the resistance which he offers! And now another case. The effectual call may be illustrated in its Sovereignty by the case of Zaccheus. Christ is entering into Jericho to preach. There is a publican living in it who is a hard, griping, grasping, miserly extortioner. Jesus Christ is coming in to call someone, for it is written He *must* abide in some man's house. Would you believe it, that the man whom Christ intends to call is the worst man in Jericho—the extortioner? He is a little short fellow and he cannot see Christ, though he has a great curiosity to look at Him. So he runs before the crowd and climbs up a sycamore tree and thinking himself quite safe amid the thick foliage, he waits with eager expectation to see this wonderful Man who had turned the world upside down. Little did he think that Christ was to turn him also! The Savior walks along preaching and talking with the people until He comes under the sycamore tree. Then lifting up His eyes, He cries—"Zaccheus, make haste and come down, for today I must abide in your house." The shot took effect, the bird fell—down came Zaccheus, invited the Savior to his house and proved that he was really called—not merely by the Voice but by Grace, itself, for he said, "Behold, Lord, the half of my goods I give unto the poor and if I have taken anything from any man by false accusation, I restore unto him fourfold." And Jesus said, "This day is salvation come unto your house." Now why call Zaccheus? There were many better men in the city than he! Why call him? Simply because the call of God comes to unworthy sinners! There is nothing in man that can deserve this call—nothing in the best of men that can invite it! God quickens whom He will and when He sends that call, though it comes to the vilest of the vile, down they come speedily and swiftly! They come down from the tree of their sin and fall prostrate in penitence at the feet of Jesus Christ!

But now to illustrate this call in its effects, we remind you that Abraham is another remarkable instance of effectual calling. "Now the Lord had said unto Abraham, get you out of your country and from your kindred and from your father's house, unto a land that I will show you" and, "by faith Abraham, when he was called to go out into a place which he should after receive for an inheritance, obeyed. And he went out, not knowing where he went." Ah, poor Abraham! As the world would have had it, what a trial his call cost him! He was happy enough in the bosom of his father's household, but idolatry crept into it and when

God called Abraham, he called him *alone* and blessed him out of Ur of the Chaldees and said to him, "Go forth, Abraham!" And he went forth, not knowing where he went. Now, when effectual calling comes into a house and singles out a man, that man will be compelled to go forth outside the camp, bearing Christ's reproach. He must come out from his very dearest friends; from all his old acquaintances; from those friends with whom he used to drink and swear and take pleasure! He must go straight away from them all to follow the Lamb wherever he goes. What a trial to Abraham's faith when he had to leave all that was so dear to him and go he knew not where! And yet God had a goodly land for him and intended to bless him greatly. Man! If you are called; if you are truly called, there will be a going out and a going out alone! Perhaps some of God's professed people will leave you. You will have to go without a solitary friend—maybe you will even be deserted by Sarah, herself, and you may be a stranger in a strange land—a solitary wanderer as all your fathers were! Ah, but if it is an *effectual* call and if salvation shall be the result thereof—what matters it though you go to Heaven alone? Better to be a solitary pilgrim to bliss, than one of the thousands who throng the road to Hell!

I will have one more illustration. When effectual calling comes to a man, at first he may not know that it is effectual calling. You remember the case of Samuel. The Lord called Samuel and he arose and went to Eli and he said, "Here am I, for you called me." Eli said, "I called not; lie down again. And he went and lay down." The second time the Lord called him and said, "Samuel, Samuel," and he arose again and went to Eli and said, "Here am I, for you did call me." And then it was that Eli, not Samuel, first of all perceived that the Lord had called the child! And when Samuel knew it was the Lord, he said, "Speak, for Your servant hears." When the work of Grace begins in the heart, the man is not always clear that it is God's work. He is impressed under the minister and, perhaps, he is rather more occupied with the impression than with the agent of the impression! He says, "I know not how it is, but I have been called. Eli, the minister, has called me." And perhaps he goes to Eli to ask what he wants with him. "Surely," he said, "the minister knew me and spoke something personally to me because he knew my case." And he goes to Eli and it is not till afterwards, perhaps, that he finds that Eli had nothing to do with the impression, but that the Lord had called him. I know this—I believe God was at work with my heart for years before I knew anything about Him. I knew there was a work. I knew I prayed and cried and groaned for mercy, but I did not know that was the Lord's work! I half thought it was my own. I did not know till afterwards, when I was led to know Christ as all my salvation and all my desire, that the Lord had called the child, for this could not have been the result of Nature—it must have been the effect of Grace.

I think I may say to those who are the beginners in the Divine Life, as long as your call is real, rest assured it is Divine! If it is a call that will suit the remarks which I am about to give you in the second part of the discourse, even though you may have thought that God's hand is not in it, rest assured that it is, for Nature could never produce effectual calling! If the call is effectual and you are brought out and brought in—brought out of sin and brought to Christ; brought out of death into life and out of slavery into liberty; then though you cannot see God's hand in it, yet, by God's Grace it is there!

II. I have thus illustrated effectual calling. And now as a matter of EXAMINATION, let each man judge himself by certain characteristics of heavenly calling which I am about to mention. If in your Bible you turn to 2 Timothy 1:9, you will read these words—"Who has saved us and called us with an holy calling." Now here is the first touchstone by which we may try our calling—many are called but few are chosen because there are many kinds of calls. But the true call, and that only, answers to the description of the text. It is "an holy calling, not according to our works, but according to His own purpose and Grace which was given us in Christ Jesus before the world began." This calling forbids all trust in our own doings and conducts us to Christ alone for salvation! And it afterwards purges us from dead works to serve the living and true God! If you are now living in sin, you are not called. If you can still continue as you were before your pretended conversion, then it is no conversion at all! That man who is called in his drunkenness, will forsake his drunkenness! Men may be called in the midst of sin, but they will not continue in it any longer. Saul was anointed to be king when he was seeking his father's donkeys— and many a man has been called when he has been seeking his own lust—but he will leave the animals and leave the lust when once he is called effectually!

Now, by this shall you know whether you are called of God or not. If you continue in sin; if you walk according to the course of this world; according to the spirit that works in the children of disobedience—then are you still dead in your trespasses and your sins. As He who has called you is holy, so must you be holy. Can you say, "Lord, You know all things; You know that I desire to keep all Your commandments and to walk blamelessly in Your sight. I know that my obedience cannot save me, but I long to obey. There is nothing that pains me so much as sin. I desire to be quit and rid of it. Lord help me to be holy."? Is that the panting of your heart? Is that the tenor of your life towards God and towards His Law? Then, Beloved, I have reason to hope that you have been called of God, for it is a holy calling with which God calls His people!

In Philippians 3:13-14 you find these words, "Forgetting those things which are behind and reaching forth unto those which are before, I press towards the mark for the prize of the high calling of God in Christ Jesus." Is then your calling a *high* calling? Has it lifted up your heart and set it upon heavenly things? Has it lifted up your hopes to hope no longer for things that are on earth, but for things that are above? Has it lifted up your tastes so that they are no longer groveling, but you choose the things that are of God? Has it lifted up the constant tenor of your life so that you spend your life with God in prayer, in praise and in thanksgiving and can no longer be satisfied with the low and mean pursuits which you followed in the days of your ignorance? Remember if you are truly called, it is a *high* calling, a calling from on High and a calling that lifts up your heart and raises it to the high things of God, eternity, Heaven and holiness!

In Hebrews 3:1, you find this sentence. "Holy brethren, partakers of the heavenly calling." Here is another test. Heavenly calling means a call from Heaven. Have you been called not of man, but of God? Can you now detect in your calling the hand of God and the voice of God? If man alone calls you, you are uncalled. Is your calling of God? And is it a call *to* Heaven as well as *from* Heaven? Can you heartily say that you can never rest satisfied till you—

"Behold His face
And never, never sin.
But from the rivers of His Grace,
Drink endless pleasures in"?

Man, unless you are a stranger here and Heaven is your home, you have not been called with a heavenly calling, for those who have been so called declare that they look for a city which has foundations whose Builder and Maker is God and they themselves are strangers and pilgrims upon the earth!

There is another test. Let me remind you that there is a passage in Scripture which may tend very much to your edification and help you in your examination. Those who are called are men who *before* the calling, groaned in sin. What says Christ?—"I came not to call the righteous, but sinners to repentance." Now, if I cannot say the first things because of shyness, though they are true, can I yet say this—that I feel myself to be a sinner; that I loathe my sinnership; that I detest my iniquity; that I feel I deserve the wrath of God on account of my transgressions? If so, then I have a hope that I may be among the called host whom God has predestinated! He has called not the righteous but *sinners* to repentance. Self-righteous Man, I can tell you in the tick of a clock, whether you have any evidence of election. I tell you— No! Christ never called the righteous! And if He has not called you and if He never does call you, you are not elect and you and your self-righteousness must be subject to the wrath of God and cast away eternally! Only the sinner, the awakened sinner, can be at all assured that he has been called. And even he, as he gets older in Grace, must look for those higher marks of the high heavenly and holy calling in Christ Jesus.

As a further test—keeping close to Scripture this morning, for when we are dealing with our own state before God there is nothing like giving the very Words of Scripture—we are told in the first Epistle of Peter, the 2nd Chapter and the 9th verse, that God has called us out of darkness into marvelous light. Is that your call? Were you once in darkness in regard to Christ? And has marvelous light manifested to you a marvelous Redeemer, marvelously strong to save? Say Soul, can you honestly declare that your past life was darkness and that your present state is Light in the Lord? "For you were sometime darkness, but now are you light in the Lord; walk as children of the light." That man is not called who cannot look back upon darkness, ignorance and sin and who cannot now say that he knows more than he did know and enjoys at times the Light of knowledge and the comfortable Light of God's Countenance.

Yet again—another test of calling is to be found in Galatians, the 5th Chapter and the 15th verse. "Brethren, you have been called into liberty." Let me ask myself again this question, "Have the fetters of my sin been broken off and am I God's free man? Have the manacles of justice been snapped and am I delivered—set free by Him who is the great Ransom of spirits?" The slave is not called. It is the free man who has been brought out of Egypt, who proves that he has been called of

God and is precious to the heart of the Most High.

And yet once more, another precious means of test is in the First of Corinthians, the 1st Chapter and the 9th verse. "He is faithful by whom you were called into the fellowship of His Son, Jesus Christ our Lord." Do I have fellowship with Christ? Do I converse with Him; commune with Him? Do I suffer *with* Him—suffer *for* Him? Do I sympathize with Him in His objectives and aims? Do I love what He loves? Do I hate what He hates? Can I bear His reproach? Can I carry His Cross? Do I tread in His steps? Do I serve His cause and is it my grandest hope that I shall see His Kingdom come; that I shall sit upon His Throne and reign with Him? If so, then I am called with the effectual calling which is the work of God's Grace and is the sure sign of my predestination!

Let me say, before I turn from this point, that it is possible for a man to know whether or not God has called him and he may know it beyond a doubt. He may know it as surely as if he read it with his own eyes—no, he may know it *more surely* than that—for if I read a thing with my eyes, even my eyes may deceive me. The testimony of sense may be false, but the testimony of the Spirit must be true! We have the witness of the Spirit within, bearing witness with our spirits that we are born of God. There is such a thing on earth as an *Infallible assurance* of our election! Let a man once get that and it will anoint his head with fresh oil; it will clothe him with the white garment of praise and put the song of the angel into his mouth! Happy, happy man who is fully assured of his interest in the Covenant of Grace, in the blood of Atonement and in the glories of Heaven! Such men there are here this very day. Let them "rejoice in the Lord always and again I say rejoice."

What would some of you give if you could arrive at this assurance? If you anxiously desire to know, you may know! If your heart pants to read its title clear, it shall do so before long. No man ever desired Christ in his heart with a living and longing desire who did not find Him sooner or later! If you have a desire, *God has given it to you!* If you pant and cry and groan after Christ, even this is His gift—bless Him for it! Thank Him for little Grace and ask Him for great Grace. He has given you hope, then ask for faith! And when He gives you faith, ask for assurance. And when you get assurance, ask for *full* assurance. And when you have obtained full assurance, ask for enjoyment. And when you have enjoyment, ask for Glory itself—and He shall surely give it to you in His own appointed season!

III. I now come to finish up with CONSOLATION. Is there anything here that can console me? Oh, yes, rivers of consolation flow from my calling! For first, if I am called, then I am predestinated, there is no doubt about it. The great scheme of salvation is like those chains which we sometimes see at horse ferries. There is a chain on this side of the river fixed into a staple and the same chain is fixed into a staple at the other side, but the greater part of the chain is for the most part under water and you cannot see it. You only see it as the boat moves on and as the chain is drawn out of the water by the force that propels the boat. If today I am enabled to say I am called, then my boat is like the ferry in the middle of the stream—I can see that part of the chain which is named, "calling," but blessed be God, that is joined to the side that is called "election," and I may also be quite clear that it is joined on to the other side, the glorious end of "glorification." If I am called, I must have been elected and I need not doubt that. God never tantalized a man by calling him by effectual Grace unless He had written that man's name in the Lamb's Book of Life! Oh, what a glorious Doctrine is that of Election, when a man can see himself to be elect! One of the reasons why many men kick against it is this—they are afraid it hurts them. I never yet knew a man who had a reason to believe that he was chosen of God, who hated the Doctrine of Election! Men hate Election just as thieves hate Chubb's patent locks! Because they cannot get at the treasure themselves they therefore hate the guard which protects it. Now election shuts up the precious treasury of God's Covenant blessings for His children only—for penitents, for seeking sinners. There are men who will not repent, will not believe— they will not go God's way—and then they grumble and growl and fret and fume because God has locked the treasure up against them. Let a man once believe that all the treasure within is his and then the stouter the bolt and the surer the lock, the better for him! Oh, how sweet it is to believe our names were on Jehovah's heart and engraved on Jesus' hands before the universe had a being! May not this electrify a man of joy and make him dance for very mirth?—

Chosen of God before time began!

Come on, slanderers! Rail on as you please! Come on, you world in arms! Cataracts of trouble descend if you will! You floods of affliction roll if so it is ordained, for God has written my name in the Book of Life! Firm as this rock I stand though nature reels and all things pass away! What consolation, then, to be called—for if I am called, then I am predestinated! Come, let us rejoice at the Sovereignty which has called us and let us remember the words of the Apostle, "For you see your calling, Brethren, how that not many wise men after the flesh, not many mighty, not many noble, are called: but God has chosen the foolish things of the world to confound the wise; and God has chosen the weak things of the world to confound the things which are mighty; and base things of the world and things which are despised, has God chosen, yes, and things which are not, to bring to nothing things that are: that no flesh should glory in His presence. But of Him are you in Christ Jesus, who of God is made unto us wisdom, and righteousness, and sanctification, and redemption: that, according as it is written, he that glories, let him glory in the Lord."

A second consolation is drawn from the grand Truth of God that if a man is called he will certainly be saved at last. To prove that, however, I will refer you to the express words of Scripture—Romans 11:29—"The gifts and calling of God are without repentance." He never repents of what He gives, nor of whom He calls! And indeed this is proven by the very Chapter out of which we have taken our text.

"Whom He did predestinate, them He also called; and whom He called, them He also justified. And whom He justified, them He also glorified," every one of them! Now, Believer, you may be very poor and very sick and very much unknown and despised, but sit down and review your calling this morning and the consequences that flow from it! As surely as you are God's called child today, your poverty shall soon be at an end and you shall be rich to all the intents of bliss! Wait awhile. That weary head shall soon be girt with a crown! Stay awhile. Those calloused hands of labor shall soon grasp the palm branch! Wipe away those tears! God shall soon wipe away your tears forever! Take away that sigh—why sigh when the everlasting song is almost on your lips? The portals of Heaven stand wide open for you. A few winged hours must fly. A few more billows must roll over you and you will be safely landed on the golden shore! Do not say, "I shall be lost. I shall be cast away." Impossible—

"Whom once He loves, He never leaves, But loves them to the end."

If He has called you, nothing can divide you from His love! The wolf of famine cannot gnaw the bond. The fire of persecution cannot burn the link; the hammer of Hell cannot break the chain! Old Time cannot devour it with rust, nor Eternity dissolve it with all its ages. Oh, believe that you are secure! That voice which called you shall call you yet again from earth to Heaven; from death's dark gloom to immortality's unuttered splendors! Rest assured the heart that called you beats with Infinite Love towards you—a love undying that many waters cannot quench and that floods cannot drown. Sit down. Rest in peace! Lift up your eyes of hope and sing your song with fond anticipation. You shall soon be with the glorified, where your portion is. You are only waiting here to be made ready for the inheritance and that done, the wings of angels shall waft you far away to the mount of peace and joy and blessedness, where—

> *"Far from a world of grief and sin,*
> *With God eternally shut in,"*

you shall rest forever and ever! Examine yourselves, then, whether you have been called. And may the love of Jesus be with you. Amen.

P

Perseverance Of the Saints

PERSEVERANCE WITHOUT PRESUMPTION

A SERMON DELIVERED ON THURSDAY
EVENING,
MARCH 7, 1872,
BY C. H. SPURGEON,

AT THE METROPOLITAN TABERNACLE,
NEWINGTON.

*"I give them eternal life,
and they shall never perish, neither
shall any man pluck them out of My hand."*
John 10:28.

THOSE of you who were present last Thursday evening will remember that I spoke upon the necessity of "holding fast the beginning of our confidence steadfast unto the end," and I showed you that it is only by continuing in the faith with which we began that we are proven to be partakers of the Lord Jesus Christ. Now, let us speak as plainly as we may, we are always liable to be misunderstood. The most eager hearer may easily confuse his thoughts with our words, and so attribute notions to us that spring up spontaneously in his own mind.

Thus I met this week with an earnest anxious inquirer who thought I had meant that though a man should be a Believer in Jesus Christ, yet after all he might perish. I dare say some expressions I used led him to think so. Had he been long a hearer here, he could not have imagined that I could give utterance to such a statement! For all of you who hear me continually know that if there is one doctrine I have preached more than any other, it is the doctrine of the Perseverance of the Saints even to the end. What I intended to say, and I do not wonder that he did not quite understand me, was this—the Believer must always be a Believer—having begun in that confidence, he must continue in that confidence.

The alternative would be that he draws back unto perdition, in which case he would perish as an unbeliever—and then the inference would be that the faith he seemed to have was a fiction, that the confidence he seemed to enjoy was a bubble—that he really never did believe to the saving of his soul. This is a fair argument based on the operation of the Spirit of God. It is in no sense a condition dependent on the good behavior of men. The one way by which a soul is saved is by that soul's abiding in Christ—if it did not abide in Christ, it would be cast forth as a branch and be withered.

But, then, we *know* that they who are grafted into Christ will abide in Christ! We reason in the manner of the Apostle Paul who, when he had spoken of the danger that some were in that, having begun well, they should end badly—after being enlightened and tasting the good Word of God and the powers of the world to come, they should turn aside—he adds, "But, Beloved, we are persuaded better things of you, and things that accompany salvation, though we thus speak."

The question, however, having been mooted, it occurs to me that it may not be unprofitable if I state briefly—not by way of controversy, but simply for the sake of instruction—the doctrine of the security of the Believer in Christ, the certainty of the Believer's perseverance even to the end, and of his entrance into eternal rest. This text at once suggests itself to me—"I give unto My sheep eternal life; and they shall never perish, neither shall any pluck them out of My hand." The three clauses of this sentence represent to us three gracious securities. Here is a Divine gift—"I *give* unto them eternal life." Here is a Divine promise, far-reaching and wide—"they shall *never* perish." And here is a Divine holdfast—"neither shall any pluck them out of My hand."

I. First, then, observe THE DIVINE GIFT—"I give unto them eternal life." Eternal life comes to every man who has it as a matter of gift. He did not possess it when he first entered into the world. He was born of the first Adam and born to die. He did not educe it or evolve it from himself by some mysterious processes. It is not a home growth, a product of the soil of humanity—it is a *gift*. Nor is eternal life bestowed as a reward for service done. It could not be—for it is a *prerequisite* to the doing of service!

The term "gift" shuts out all idea of debt. If it is a gift, or of Divine Grace, then it is no more of debt or of reward. Wherever eternal life is implanted in any person's soul it is the free gift of the Lord Jesus Christ—not deserved but *bestowed* on the unworthy. Therefore we see no reason why it should be revoked from the person who has received it. For, suppose there are certain disqualifications in the man who has participated in the gift, yet they cannot otherwise operate to his prejudice in enjoying the gift than they would have operated to his ever receiving it if they had been taken into account at all.

The thing does not come to him because of any worthiness in him, but comes as a gratuity. There is no reason why it should not continue, since it has come into existence, or why the present tense, as we have it here, should not always be a present fact. "I give"—I continue to give—"to them eternal life," that cannot be affected by an unworthiness subsequently discovered because God knows the end from the beginning. When He bestowed eternal life upon the man who has it, He knew right well every imperfection and failing that would occur in that man. These demerits, had they been reasons at all, would have been a cause for the *not* giving, rather than for giving and then taking away again.

It is inconsistent with the gifts of God for them ever to be disannulled. We have it laid down as a rule of the kingdom of which there is no violation, that, "the gifts and calling of God are without repentance." He does not rescind in caprice that which He has conferred of His own good will. It is not according to the royal Nature of the Lord our God to bestow a gift of Grace upon a soul and then afterwards to withdraw it—to lift up a man from his natural degradation and set him among princes by endowing him with eternal life, and then to cast him down from his high estate by depriving him of all the infinite benefits He has conferred.

The very language I am using is contradictory enough of itself to refute the suggestion. To give *eternal* life is to give a life beyond the contingencies of this present mortal existence. "Forever" is stamped on the charter. To take it away is not consistent with the royal bounty of the King of kings, even if it were possible that such a thing could be. "I give unto them eternal life." If He gives, then, He gives with the sovereignty and generosity of a king. He gives permanently, on an enduring tenure. He gives so that He will not revoke the grant. He gives and it is theirs—it shall be theirs by Divine charter forever and ever.

We may infer the certain safety of the Believer, not only from the fact that this life is an absolute gift and will not, therefore, be withdrawn, but from the nature of the gift, it being *eternal* life. "I give unto My sheep eternal life." "Yes, but," says somebody, "they lose it." Then they cannot have had *eternal* life. It is a mistake in terms to say that a man has *eternal* life and yet perishes. Can death befall the *immortal*, or change affect the *immutable*, or decay corrode the *imperishable*? How can life be *eternal* if it comes to an end? How can it be possible that one shall have *eternal* life and yet die with sudden shock, or drop as feeble Nature fails of all her functions?

No! *Eternity* is not to be measured by weeks or months or years! When Christ says *eternal*, He means *eternal*, and if I have received the gift of *eternal life*, it is not possible for me to sin so as to lose that spiritual life by any means whatever. "It is eternal life." We may reasonably expect the Believer to hold on to the end, because the life which God has implanted within him is of that Nature that it must continue to exist, must conquer all difficulties, must ripen, must perfect, must cast out sin from him and must bring him to eternal Glory! When Christ spoke by the well to the Samaritan woman, he said, "Whoever drinks of the water that I shall give him shall never thirst; but the water that I shall give him shall be in him a well of water springing up into everlasting life."

This cannot mean a transient draught that would slake the thirst for an hour or two—it must imply such a partaking as changes a man's actual constitution and his destiny—and become in him a never-failing wellspring. The life which God implants in Believers by *regeneration* is not like the life which we now possess by *generation.* This mortal life *does* pass away. It is connected with flesh and all flesh is like grass—it withers. "That which is born of the flesh is flesh." Not so the new life that is born of the Spirit and it is Spirit, and Spirit is not capable of destruction—it shall continue and last on, world without end. The eternal life within every man who has it was begotten in him "not of the will of man, nor of flesh, nor of blood, but of God" Himself.

Thanks be unto the Father, for it is of Him that we are "begotten again unto a lively hope by the resurrection of Jesus Christ from the dead." Tracing this implanted life to its germ, we are said to be "born again, not of corruptible seed, but of incorruptible, by the word of God, which lives and abides forever." It is a holy seed. It cannot sin, for it is born of God. We are made partakers of the Divine Nature, and the *new life* within us is a Divine life. It is the life of God within the soul of man! We become the twice-born, with a life that can no more die than the life of God Himself, for it is, in fact, a spark from that great central Sun—it is a new well in the soul which draws its supplies from the deep that lies under— from the inexhaustible fountain of the fullness of God! This, then, is a second reason for believing in the security and final perseverance of the Believer. He has a gift from Christ, and Christ will not withdraw His gift—he has a life which is in itself immortal and *eternal.*

But further, this life within the Believer which is a gift from Christ is always in connection *with* Christ. We live because we are *one* with Christ—as the branch sucks its sap from the vine—so do we continue to derive our life's blood, our life's supplies, from Christ Himself. The union between the Believer and Christ is vital and, to the fullest degree, assuring. For what does our Lord say of it?—"Because I live, you shall live also." It is not a partnership which may be dissolved or a connection which may be severed—it is a necessity that no accident can interfere with! It is a fixed law of being—"because I live, you shall live also."

That the union between Christ and His people is indissoluble appears obvious from the figures which are used to illustrate it. To such an overwhelming extent do they denote that there can be no separation, that we may well say, "Who shall separate us from the love of God which is in Christ Jesus our Lord?" Are we not married to Christ? What metaphor could be more expressive? To estimate its value you must take the Divine account of the relationship. Although weddings are secularized by our Acts of Parliament, and nuptial ties are looked upon as civil contracts, *God* has pronounced man and wife to be one flesh! Yes, in the sight of Heaven, he that is joined to a harlot is one body with her.

In ordinary marriage, divorce is possible, and, alas, too common—but when you come to Scripture, you find it written that He hates putting away. He has said, "I will betroth you unto Me forever, I have betrothed you unto Myself in righteousness and in faithfulness, and you shall know the Lord." The marriage between our souls and Christ can never be dissolved! It were blasphemy to suppose that Christ shall appeal for a divorce, or that there should be a proclamation made that He has put away that spouse whom He chose of old, for whom He has prepared the great wedding feast and for whose eternal bliss He has gone to Glory to prepare a place! No, we cannot imagine such espousals leading to a separation!

Again, are we not members of His body? Shall Christ be dismembered? Shall He, every now and then, lose one limb or another? Can you suppose that Christ is maimed? I scarcely like to think, much less to *express* the thought, of here or there an eye, or a foot or an ear needed to complete the perfection of His mystic Person. No! It shall not be! Members of the body of Christ shall be so vitally quickened by the heart, and by Himself, the Head, that they shall continue to live because He lives! When a man stands in water, the flood might naturally have power to drown him, but as long as his head remains above water, the stream cannot possibly drown his feet or his hands! And because Christ, the Head, cannot die, cannot be destroyed, all the floods that shall come upon the members of His body shall not—*cannot*—destroy them!

Moreover, the life of the Believer is constantly sustained by the indwelling of the Holy Spirit. It is a matter of fact under the Gospel dispensation that not only is the Holy Spirit *with* Believers but He is *in* Believers. He dwells in them! He makes them His temple! The life, as we have shown you, is "sui generis," of its own kind, *immortal.* It is immortal because it is united with an undying Christ—but it is also immortal because it is supported by a Divine Spirit who cannot be overcome. The Holy Spirit has power to meet all the mischief of false and evil spirits that aim at our destruction, and, from day to day adds fresh fuel to the eternal flame of the Believer's life within. Were it not for the Holy Spirit's abiding with us, we might be the subjects of some doubt, but as long as He continues to abide with us forever, we will not fear.

The first consolation that we thus draw from the text is that we are the recipients of a Divine *gift*—"I *give* unto My sheep eternal life."

II. Now, secondly, we have added to this, A DIVINE PROMISE—"They shall never perish." I am very thankful for this Word because there have been some who have tried to do away with the force of the entire passage—"neither shall any pluck them out of My hand." "No," they have said, "but they may slip between His fingers, and though they cannot be plucked out, yet they may go out on their own accord." But here is a short sentence that puts all such thoughts out of the question—"they shall never perish"—*in* His hands or *out* of His hands, under any supposition whatever—"they shall never perish"!

Observe that there is no restriction here—it includes all time. "They shall never perish." Are they young Believers? Are their passions strong? Are their judgments weak? Have they little knowledge, small experience, and tender faith? May they not die while yet they are lambs and perish while they are so feeble? "They shall never perish." But, in middle life, when men too often lose the freshness of early Grace, when the love of their espousals may, perhaps, have lost its power, may they not get worldly? May they not, somehow or other, then be led aside? "They shall never perish." "They shall *never* perish."

Perish they would, could worldliness destroy them! Perish they would, could evil utterly and entirely get the mastery of Grace—but it shall not. "They shall never perish!" But, may they not grow older, and yet not wiser? May they not be surprised by temptation, as so many have been in times when they have become carnally secure, because they thought their experience had made them strong? "They shall never perish"—neither if they are beginners, nor if they have all but finished their course. "They shall *never* perish." It shuts out all time—all reference to time—by taking the whole range of possible periods into the one word, "never." "They shall *never* perish."

No less does the sweep of the sentence include all contingencies. "They shall never perish." What? Not if they are severely tempted? "They shall never perish." Not if they backslide? They shall be restored again. "They shall never perish." But, if they continue in backsliding and die so? Ah, that they shall not do—"They shall *never* perish." You must not suppose that which never can occur. "They shall *never* perish." They shall never get into such a condition that they shall be utterly without Divine Grace—they shall never be in such a state of heart that sin shall have dominion over them—utter and entire dominion.

It may come in; it may seem for a time to get the mastery, but sin shall never have dominion over them that they shall perish before the Lord. "They shall *never* perish." It takes in all the flock. "*They* shall never perish"—that is, not one of His sheep. This is not the distinctive privilege of a *few*, but the common mercy of them all! None of them—not one of them—

shall ever perish. If you, Believer in Christ, are the most obscure of all the family, you shall never perish. If you have, indeed, received the inner life and true Grace is in your soul, though no one knows your name and no one lends you a helping hand—though, as a solitary pilgrim you should walk the heavenly road all alone, weak and feeble, and trembling all the way—yet you shall never perish! The promise is not to *some*, but to *all* the believing sheep of Christ. "They shall never perish."

And, Beloved, it may greatly strengthen our faith and sweetly revive our spirits if we consider how this doctrine harmonizes with other doctrines which are most surely believed among us. Christ's sheep were of old chosen of God unto salvation. But if they perished, the election of God would be frustrated! From the foundation of the world He appointed them that they should bring forth fruit unto holiness, even unto the end, and, if they do not, how can His will be done on earth as it is in Heaven? They were a people set apart unto Himself that they might honor Him by good works, if they failed of this, if they fell from their blest estate, if they did utterly perish, the Father's counsel would be foiled—and that cannot be!

The purpose of God secures their final perseverance. "They shall never perish." We may rest assured that they shall be preserved because of the effectual redemption which Christ has worked out for them. We believe, Beloved, in this place, (though the doctrine is very much disparaged nowadays), in an *actual* and *literal* substitutionary Sacrifice. We believe that Jesus died for His people, and—

"Bore, that they might never bear
The Father's righteous ire."

Now, if He paid their debts, they have no debts to discharge! If He has borne their punishment, they have no penalty to suffer. If He stood in their place, Justice as well as Grace—Justice and Grace together—demand that they should be saved. Jesus Christ has offered for them an Atonement—and, "who is he that condemns?" "It is Christ that died, yes, rather that has risen again."

"If, when we were enemies, we were reconciled to God by the death of His Son, much more, being reconciled, we shall be saved by His life." If He died to bear our guilt, much more, the Atonement being completed, shall we enter into the fullness of rest! If He would not lose us, viewing us as unredeemed, but came and paid the price, much less will He lose us now that He has redeemed us unto God, by His blood, out of every nation and people and kindred and tongue. He laid down His life for His sheep. He loved the Church and gave Himself for it that He might present it unto Himself a glorious Church—and He will effect the purpose for which He has already ventured so much. He will surely claim and as surely receive at the hand of Justice the salvation of those for whom He was a vicarious Victim.

Furthermore, dear Friends, he that believes in Christ is justified from all things from which he could not be justified by the Law of Moses. Is it according to the manner of man, first to justify, and afterwards to condemn? Certainly not! But if it were, it is not according to the supreme equity of the Most High God! Has He pronounced a man just? That man is just. When He has declared the man's transgressions forgiven, shall they be again reckoned to him?—again laid to his door? Is it not said that He has put away our sins like a cloud, and will He gather the cloud of yesterday again?

Has He not said He has cast our sins into the depths of the sea? Shall that which Jehovah Himself has consigned to the oblivious ocean be washed up again as though He had only committed it to the shallows? As far as the East is from the West, so far has He removed our transgressions from us! Our East and West are wide enough apart—but what must *God's* East and West be when He looks through infinite space? He has removed those sins so far from us that the swiftest-footed devil could not bring them back again though he had a whole eternity to perform the feat. He has put them away forever!

Yes, hear what is said of the Messiah—"He has finished transgression, made an end of sin, and brought in everlasting righteousness." If it is finished, it is finished, and if He has made an end of it, where is it? Where is it? "If it is searched for it shall not be found"—yes, it shall not be, says the Lord. O Beloved, how, then, shall the man that believes in Christ be condemned—condemned for sin that has been pardoned? How shall he be cast into Hell? For what? For offenses that have been borne by the Savior? How shall he be condemned whom God has justified? Give no countenance to the thought! Let no fear nor fancy induce you to lend an ear to the suggestion! The sentence of remission once passed upon a man stands irrevocable. "It is God that justifies; who is he that condemns?"

In the Believer, moreover, there is a work of God begun which He has engaged to complete. It has never been said of God that He began to build and was not able to finish. "We are persuaded that He which has begun a good work in you will carry it on and perfect it to the Day of Christ." It has not been according to Jehovah's habit to leave unfinished His works—why *should* He leave them unfinished? Is there a need of power? Inconceivable! Is there a need of will? We cannot imagine it—for if His will has changed there must be some reason for the change. And if it is so, is God wiser than He was? Has he altered His plan because He has discovered some error in it? If not, if Infinite Wisdom led Him to put His hand to it, Infinite Wisdom will *keep* His hand to the work—

> ***"The work which Wisdom undertakes,***
> ***Eternal Mercy ne'er forsakes."***

O Beloved, the very beginning of the work from God foretells that the work will be fully carried out!

The doctrine of Adoption supplies us with yet another argument for our safety. Every man who is saved, justified, forgiven, is also *adopted* into the family of God. And do you think that God shifts and changes His children who are called by His own name? Do you imagine such a thing credible? Does it sound like a fact? Are you your Father's child today and somebody else's child tomorrow? Is not the absurdity too obvious to need refutation?

No—I know not where could have come so whimsical a thought as that we should be children of God today, and by-and-by children of the devil—changing, thus, the blessed paternity which God Himself claims as to all His people.

"But, we may play the prodigal," says one. Yes, I answer, and we may be brought back again after we have gone astray as the prodigal was. Besides, the prodigal was still a *son*—even when at the swine trough, and when he had wasted all his substance in riotous living—he was still beloved of the father. And because he was a son he came back again with weeping and bitterness of spirit, and found peace and pardon. Had he been no son, he might, like others, have spent his living with harlots and there had been no saying, "I will arise and go unto my father." But Grace operated on his heart—he was quickened mysteriously, and he said—"I must leave this life of poverty and sin and go back to my father's house."

And, if God's child shall go astray, as it is possible, (only God grant you and I never may), yet there is a voice that says, "Return, return you backsliding Israel! I am married unto you, says the Lord." Adoption is surely a grand proof that the Lord's people shall be kept and preserved—that there shall be an unbroken family of God in Heaven. He shall not have to lament that His own dear sons and daughters, begotten by His Grace, have utterly perished. Jesus shall say, "Here am I and the children You have given Me."

III. And, now, the last point is THE DIVINE HOLDFAST—"None shall pluck them out of My hand." Then all the saints are in Jesus' hands! They are not only in His heart, but in His hands—just as the high priests wore the names of the 12 tribes on the breastplates, and wore them on the shoulders also. The power, as well as the affection of Christ shall preserve the people of God. They are in His hands. "All Your saints are in Your hands." What a blessed place for us to be in—in the hands of Christ—always there!

But does not our Lord intimate as if to forewarn us that a great many attempts would be made to pluck us out of those hands? Satan would do it—our own base lusts would do it— the ungodly would do it. The very air is full of tempters who would, if they could, pluck us away from Christ. We have, therefore, cause for great watchfulness, deep humility, but also for much *thankfulness* that we are placed where the tempters cannot reach us, for the promise assures us that none is able to pluck us out of Christ's hand! There is not power enough in legions of fallen spirits, if they were marshaled in battle array against one poor weak Christian, to snatch him away from Christ!

Yes, should they besiege him without intermission like a vast herd of lions seeking to devour one lamb, the defense were so much stronger than the invasion that they could not pluck even that one out of Christ's hands! The Destroyer has never yet celebrated a triumph over the Redeemer! He is not able to hold up a single jewel of the Redeemer's crown and say, "Aha! Aha! I stole it from Your diadem! You could not keep it!" He has no single sheep there to which he can point and say, "Ah, Shepherd of the sheep, You could not keep them all! The strong were safe enough—they helped themselves, but this poor weakling could not help itself—and You could not help it. Lo! I have borne it away from You! Your flock, which is Your pride, is not complete! You Yourself, as Shepherd, have a spot upon Your name, for You have lost at least this one that Your Father gave You and whom You have purchased with Your blood!"

It cannot be! It shall not be! The powers of darkness have conspired for this and struggled for this, but they have not yet prevailed, nor shall they! "None shall pluck them out of My hand." Oh, rest in the hands of Christ, rest quietly—now that you are there you are secure, neither shall any pluck you away. As if He would make assurance doubly sure, and give us a very strong consolation, He added, "My Father which gave them Me is greater than all, and none shall pluck them out of My Father's hand." You can interpret the figure. There was Christ's hand and His people in it, and He shall shut it fast to hold them. But that hand was pierced once, and so to make it doubly sure, the Father clasps it with *His* hand, and so within a double encircling the elect of God are held and embraced!

There is the pierced hand of Jesus and there is the Father's almighty hand—so there are two hands to protect and defend them. Well may they, now, cheerfully defy all power—terrestrial or infernal—to ever destroy them. They shall forever rest in perfect security beneath the guardian care of the Man Mediator, Christ the Lord, and God the everlasting and ever blessed Father, who also takes them into His sacred keeping! Do I hear anyone object, saying, "Well, but if this is true, then may not a man live as he likes?" Sir, how can you ask that question? What do you mean by it? Do you mean, "May a man live in *sin*?" I have been trying to show that if a man is one of Christ's sheep, he cannot perish, by which I mean, he cannot *live in sin*—for that is to perish!

When I maintain that he *cannot* live in sin as he did, and cease to be a gracious man—do you ask me whether he will not, therefore, sin willfully because he is saved from his sins? You must surely misunderstand me! "But, may not a man fall? Now I have these checks taken from me, I may grow wanton." What checks? If I lay it down that a man who is enlisted as a soldier is always a soldier, how can you tell me I have taken away some checks? I see not how that can be! I have rather implied a great many strong incentives to virtue than offered a single pretext for vice. Certainly he is not to lay down his commission because he is enlisted for life in the service of his Lord!

If he ever did lay it down, he never could take it up again. Could these fall away, it were impossible, again, to renew them to repentance. If God's work did fail, if Christ's atoning blood did fall short of its aim, there would remain no hope for them. The ground on which the dew that moistens the flowers descends—when it yields nothing but thorns and briars—is given up as worthless. Were a man in some fit of enthusiasm to profess that he believed the Gospel, and then take a fit of liberty and plunge into dissipation you would all know what to think of his sincerity. When the guilt of sin is removed, the love of sin is purged out of the *heart*—and when the Spirit of holiness is given, the *love* of holiness is infused into the heart. The man who truly believes begins a life of *holiness*, and from that life of holiness he will never utterly depart.

I grant you he may be overtaken in a fault. He may be surprised with a temptation. He may stumble through weakness, or through lack of watchfulness—but he will be led back again into repentance—he shall *not* be allowed to *perish*. The life that is in him is *immortal*—a holy incorruptible seed—and it will continue to develop in spite of sultry heat or biting frost, blight or mildew, till it blooms in the perfection of life above. Says one, "Ah, Sir, I hold no argument about your doctrine. My fear is for myself—I do not think I should live as I now do if I were not afraid of falling away." Is not that a suitable fear for the child of the bondwoman—"Unless I do so-and-so I shall be sent into the wilderness with my mother Hagar." Very likely you will!

But I know this, I am the child of the freewoman, that is Sarah, and I know my Father will never send His child into the wilderness. What then? Shall His attachment provoke my alienation? Shall I act shamefully because He appoints me to honor? No, no, but because He loves *me* so, I will love Him in return! I pray Him to forgive my offenses, but I will seek to do all that is possible to show that I realize the greatness of His love and desire to make some poor return for it as best I can. "Well, but," says somebody, "are we not admonished with warnings against falling away?" Certainly, and they are the most terrible that language can describe. Undoubtedly the Scripture paints the pilgrim's path as full of peril. It is not by creature strength that we can hold our own!

Could the precious blood lose its virtue—did the blessed Spirit withdraw His influence— were the timely succor withheld, we have no resources! For all manner of sin there is a remedy—believe in Christ as a Savior—but for apostasy there is no cure. If you trample on the one Sacrifice, no second sacrifice will ever be offered. There is but one new birth. Regeneration is once and once only. "But why these warnings," you say, "if it cannot happen?" Remember God does not deal with His people as if they were blocks of wood or iron cast and run into a mold. We are *beings* with a will and a judgment, and God deals with us in that way.

Now, if I have poison in my house and it should be necessary for some reason or other that poison should be there, I do not intend that my children should ever have that poison or take it. Suppose me to be Omnipotent and that I have power to prevent their taking it, yet I do not lock it up and put it where they could not possibly get it? I put it where they can get it if they like, and it will kill them if they do get it—but I tell them they must not take it. I describe to them the results that will follow, and I have such a loving power over my children's hearts—(suppose it to be so)—that they do not disobey me so as to take this poison. Though it is there and devils come into the house and tempt them to take it, yet they will not take it but put it from them. I should thus be making an exhibition to those who looked on, of the love to me that was in my children's hearts, and also of my power over my children's hearts, though I did not violate their wills and did not make it impossible for them to destroy themselves.

Now, it is so here. Sin is permitted to be in the world—I do not know why—and God does not render it impossible for a man to go and commit any sin. The man might—he would—unless God's Grace prevented. But God's Grace is not mechanical in its action. It is not like a fetter, or a chain. It is not, (as I have heard some say), *dragging* people to Heaven by their ears. No, it is a mighty force—an Omnipotent power—but quite consistent with free agency. It never operates contrary to the laws of mind, and God is glorified in this—that though His children are thus tempted, they do not run into fatal soul-destroying sin! They do not go into such apostasy from Him as would be final and prove altogether destructive.

They are kept by His gracious power—kept as men—drawn, but with cords of love—bound, but with the bands of a man. Do you object that "good men fall?" Good men do *not* fall so as to *perish*. Good men *do* fall, for they are men! But, the truly gracious man with all his sins, repents, still believes, and with broken bones goes back to his Lord and proves himself to be still a child. The sheep may fall into a ditch—it will not roll in the mire as a hog would if it fell there. A sheep, even when it falls into a ditch, proves that it is a sheep still. There is a difference in the *nature* of it.

When I have seen a child of God fall into sin, I have known that if he were a child of God he would hate himself for it; he would grieve over it, and could not be at peace and ease in it. Do you tell me of a Christian who lived in sin and seemed very happy? Be sure that he was *not* a Christian but a pretender! He who can continue in sin and delight in it is no child of God! He that can go day after day into vice or can tolerate in himself any known sin has a spot which is not the spot of God's children. He has a mark upon him which never was and never shall be upon a truly quickened child of God! "Be you holy, for I am holy," is the voice which sounds in the saint's ear, and if he does not always obey it as he should, this is the complaining of his soul—and it makes him go weeping and lamenting before his God. But still, in the main, it ever shall be the righteous shall hold on his way, and he that has clean hands shall wax stronger and stronger.

I have one word for any here who are unconverted but would desire salvation. Do you know, dear Friends, that one of the great leading thoughts of my young life, the master thought that brought me to the Savior, was belief in the doctrine of final perseverance? Perhaps you wonder how that could be, but so it was. I saw while yet I was a lad many promising boys and lads who made total shipwreck early in their lives by falling into gross vices. I felt in my soul a loathing of the sins which I heard they had committed. I had been kept from them by Divine counsels, by gracious interpositions, by parental teaching and by pious example. Still I feared lest the sins into which these young men had fallen might master me. Such knowledge as I had of the depravity of my own heart led me to distrust myself.

I was convinced that unless I was converted, born again, and received the new life, I had no safeguard. Whatever good resolutions I might make, the probabilities were that they would be good for nothing when temptation assailed me. I might be like those of whom it has been said, "They see the Devil's hook and yet cannot help nibbling at his bait." But that I should morally disgrace myself, as some had done whom I had known and heard of, was a hazard from the very *thought* of which I shrunk with horror. When I heard and read with wondering eyes that whoever believed in Christ Jesus should be saved, the Truth of God came to my heart with a welcome I cannot describe to you. The doctrine that He would keep the feet of His saints had a charm, indeed, for me!

I thought, "Then if I go to Jesus and get from Him a new heart and a right spirit, I shall be secured against these temptations into which others have fallen. I shall be preserved by Him." I do not say *that* drove me to Christ—a sense of *sin* did that—but it attracted me to Him. It was one of the beauties of His face that ravished me—that He was a faithful Keeper of all souls that were committed to Him—that He was able and willing to take the young man and make him cleanse his way and keep him even to the end! O young people, there is no life assurance like a believing in Jesus Christ!—

**_"Grace shall preserve your following years,
And make your virtues strong."_**

I do not preach to you tonight of a sandy foundation that will give way under your feet, but a Rock to which you may continually retreat—in which you may always dwell secure. I do not present to you a salvation that may fail you under some stress of temptation, but a salvation that is strong, having in it "the sure mercies of David." He that believes and is baptized shall be saved—saved from sinning, from the *guilt* as well as the *punishment* of sin, and brought to Heaven holy and meet for the inheritance of the saints. God grant you to believe in Christ. Amen, and amen!

ABOUT THE AUTHOR

Charles Haddon (C. H.) Spurgeon, was born on June 19, 1834, in Kelvedon, Essex, and died on January 31, 1892. He started preaching when he was 15. He married Susannah Thompson in 1856, and their twin sons, Thomas and Charles, were born on September 20, 1857. He has been called the "Prince of Preachers," and his sermons are among the best in Christian literature.

ΩΩΩΩΩΩΩΩΩΩΩΩΩΩΩ

C. H. Spurgeon stated in his autobiography:

"I have my own private opinion that there is no such thing as preaching Christ and Him crucified unless we preach what nowadays is called Calvinism; it is a nickname to call it Calvinism; Calvinism is the gospel and nothing else. I do not believe we can preach the gospel if we do not preach justification by faith without works; nor unless we preach the sovereignty of God in His dispensation of grace; nor unless we exalt the electing, unchangeable, eternal, immutable, conquering love of Jehovah; nor do I think we can preach the gospel unless we base it upon the special and particular redemption of His elect and chosen people which Christ wrought out upon the cross; nor can I comprehend a gospel which lets saints fall away after they are called, and suffers the children of God to be burned in the fires of damnation after having once believed in Jesus."